H. A. IRONSIDE
MEMORIAL LIBRARY

LIBRARY
BRYAN COLLEGE
DAYTON, TN. 37321

To our very dear friend
on the occasion of her
birthday. Feb. 23. 1936.

L. G. & E. J. Pudney.

AMBASSADORS FOR CHRIST

AMBASSADORS
FOR CHRIST

By

MILDRED CABLE

and

FRANCESCA FRENCH

LIBRARY
BRYAN COLLEGE
DAYTON, TN. 37321

LONDON
HODDER AND STOUGHTON, LIMITED

First Printed	.	.	.	January	1935
Reprinted	.	.	.	February	1935
Reprinted	.	.	.	April	1935
Reprinted	.	.	.	July	1935
Reprinted	.	.	.	December	1935

PRINTED IN GREAT BRITAIN FOR HODDER & STOUGHTON, LTD.
BY WYMAN & SONS, LTD., LONDON, FAKENHAM AND READING.

11449

The Reason for Writing this Book.

DURING the period of a prolonged furlough the writers of this book have been cross-questioned by scores of young people, as to the missionary calling, its demands and its problems, and also regarding the attitude of organised Societies toward the missionary applicant.

They have received many letters asking for help and advice, of which the following is the most comprehensive. It must be admitted that a man is seldom ready for an answer until he has asked the question but, once he has done so, that question demands a reply which is honest and unequivocal.

This is the spirit in which the writers have tried to do their work. If any of the answers seem to be ambiguous, or if any important question has been overlooked, they pledge themselves to meet further inquiry with the directness that so sacred a subject demands.

MILDRED CABLE,
FRANCESCA FRENCH.

The Willow Cottage,
    Stour Row,
        Shaftesbury,
            Dorset.

One of the Letters to which this Book is the Reply.

Dear Miss Cable,

I have been meaning to write to you for some time to ask a question which has been troubling me and several of my friends for some years.

Ever since your visit to us I have been convinced that you, perhaps more than anyone else I have ever met, have the necessary knowledge and experience to deal with the problem.

Why do missionary speakers say so very little about the difficult side of their work?

Is there really another side of which we hear practically nothing? If so, why are we not told?

What are the true reactions and feelings of a young missionary at each of the following stages:

(*a*) When he has just arrived on the field?

(*b*) After the romantic glamour has had time to wear off?

(*c*) When the language question is overcome and he is faced with those forces of evil to which we hear speakers refer in vague terms?

A Deputational Secretary of one of the well-known Evangelical Societies, after a very straight talk had been given by a colleague (in which he stressed the fact that a missionary's life was no " picnic ") said to me : " I wish —— had not spoken as he did ; there will be no volunteers if he goes on those lines."

The question that immediately came to my mind was : " . . . . Why not tell the whole truth ? "

In the legal profession the oath that is familiar to us incorporates the words : " The Truth, the whole Truth, and nothing but the Truth." Surely in this most important question of the choice of our vocation in life, we are entitled to know the whole truth. A half truth is as bad as a lie. Can it be that Societies to-day are guilty of such a sin against the younger generation, as to hide from them the real cost of their calling ?

What is the real truth ? I should be very grateful if you could answer these questions somehow— perhaps in the book which I hear you are writing— for they are questions which go right to the root of things in the practical aspect of a young Christian's life.

I hope I have not been too straight in writing as I have done, but what I have said is simply the honest impression I have gained and the problem which I am facing after having listened to dozens of excellent missionary addresses.

Yours sincerely,

" *Does the road wind up-hill all the way ?*
  Yes, to the very end.
  Will the day's journey take the whole long day ?
  From morn to night, my friend."

NOTE.—For purposes of convenience the masculine gender is used throughout this book. Let the word "man" be understood in the sense of "genus homo."

CONTENTS

Contents

The Ambassador—His Credentials

THE burning, acrid desert sands of Mongolia had given way to pasture lands, where thousands of heads of cattle grazed, under the control of mounted herdsmen who rounded up the beasts and drove them from one part of the prairie to another.

On this quiet, spring morning there was unusual excitement among the herdsmen, for with their keen, telescopic eyes they had sighted a strange caravan approaching from the South. It was still many miles away, but was evidently moving in their direction.

There was nothing alarming in the appearance of the cavalcade, but who could tell of what it might be the vanguard? The far-reaching call of the desert rangers quickly brought other herdsmen to the scene, and together the riders watched the progress of the slowly advancing caravan. There was rapid talk in anxious tones as the startled men discussed the situation. Political agents? Surveyors of the land? Tax collectors? Travellers from strange lands come to spy out the country?

" To the Prince ! " shouted the leader, and one rider wheeled his horse and galloped out of sight, while others adroitly chased the cattle toward a more distant pasture. From the Prince's encampment, hidden among the tamarisks, more riders appeared, each with a rifle slung on his back. All galloped forward, spread out, then converged toward the caravan, skilfully encircling it.

A detachment of armed men rode forward, and the caravan halted :

" Who are you, and where are you from ? "

Salutations were exchanged, and while the talk continued, two riders galloped back to the Chief to report that a party of holy women, on pilgrimage, asked leave to pitch a tent near the water, and graze their beasts on the pasture land.

Gradually, fear gave place to curiosity, and when the " holy women " reached the camping ground, they were surrounded by a band of inquisitive tribesmen, anxious to talk, eager to ask questions, and keen to inspect them and their belongings. By the time the camp was pitched, everyone was friendly, and the riders dismounted to help by holding the posts, and tightening the ropes. The tents were near grass and water, but at a respectful distance from the royal enclosure.

Early next day the Prince's Interpreter appeared, speaking fluent Chinese, and commanded by his Mongol master, to convey thanks for the offering of holy books and choice food. He was also bearer of a message requesting the "holy women's" attendance at the Encampment. It was a hot day, and the party toiled with considerable fatigue, through loose sand, to the group of tents hidden behind a palisade.

The Audience Tent was a very large one, and the Prince sat in the chief place on the dais, with the foreign visitors at his right hand, and a tall Living

Buddha on the left. At the lower end of the tent the Interpreter knelt, facing him. Standing in the background, was the assembled household, staring at the unusual sight.

The Prince himself was a fine manly figure, wearing a green brocade coat with a high scarlet collar. His gestures were imperious, and he sat with knees far apart, his feet in high leather boots turned up at the toes and stitched in many colours. The thick hands which rested on his knees, were laden with massive rings.

" When did you leave Russia ? " he began. " What, not Russians ? English, did you say ? "

" Their country lies West, beyond Hindustan," quietly said the Living Buddha.

" I suppose your King has sent you here, and will meet all your expenses," continued the Prince.

" We are here by order of the God of Heaven, not by that of the King of our country," said the women.

" Are their husbands with them ? What I Unmarried ? "

" They are holy women," said the Living Buddha, " and they are vowed to celibacy. They do good works, and travel about teaching their religion."

" Excellent, excellent," said the Prince, raising his two thumbs in sign of great approbation. Then lifting a volume from the packet at his side : " I have been reading these books, which are the same as those used by the Reds," he said. " You have only one more stage from here, to the Russian border station, and there you will gain many converts."

Whereupon, raising his voice, he shouted an order, and there instantly appeared a sinister-looking man in Lama dress, who casually handled the Gospels and declared :

" These are certainly the same books as those read in Moscow, and they teach the community of goods. A very good doctrine, too—no poor, no rich, and plenty for everyone."

In this difficult atmosphere, three of Christ's Ambassadors endeavoured to proclaim some of the main truths of Christianity, while the Prince nodded his warrior head in approbation, and the tall, grey-haired, ascetic Living Buddha listened intently. Meanwhile, the sinister Lama sneered and grinned like an evil genius.

This was a crucial hour for the Prince, whose whole life was governed by reference to the spirit world, and who would undertake nothing without an offering at the *obo*, to pacify the malignant intentions of the demons, for he was simultaneously faced with two conflicting statements :

" There is one true God, and He commands men, everywhere, to repent, and offers them remission of sins through the Saviour," proclaimed the Ambassadors of Christ.

" There is no God," said the protagonist of atheism.

Two hours passed in talk, then, in a pause of the conversation, a new subject occurred to the Chief, and he asked to see the visitors' passports. They were produced, and the Prince, the Interpreter, the Living Buddha and the Wicked Lama, all bent their heads intently, scrutinising the fascinating documents and verifying each word of their contents. It was well that the national passports were in order, and that each *visa* was correct, but these missionary ambassadors were gloriously conscious that their supreme credentials, issued by the One and Only Potentate, and written in His Word, lay unrecognised at the heathen monarch's side :

" Go ye into all the world and preach the gospel to every creature, and lo, I am with you alway, even unto the end of the age."

" As Christ's Ambassadors, we speak ; God, as it were, making entreaty through us : we entreat you, on Christ's behalf, be reconciled to God."

IT was a congenial circle that sat talking on a chilly afternoon in May, around an open fire in the old country house. It held people of various nationalities, and their conversation was concerned with international affairs. They were a trustworthy group, and even the Chargé d'Affaires was not afraid to express himself among them.

"Things could not look blacker than they do in our country. We are up against a formidable foe this time," said a young Easterner, speaking in his own tongue.

"Do not despair, things may come out all right," said another, "for they have found a big man to handle the situation. He is the strong personality to whom everyone looks in this contingency."

"I think that you are quite wrong," said the Chargé d'Affaires. "The person you refer to is not a big man at all; in fact he is of quite ordinary ability, and only big because of the standing of the one he represents."

The conversation went on, but the missionary who sat in the corner ceased to follow it. That sentence: "He is not a big man at all—only big because of the man he represents," had started a train of thought. Here was the peculiar honour of the missionary's calling expressed in a sentence—only big because of

Him Whom he represents. That's it, it is all that a man stands for that makes him so important, that gives such weight to everything he says, so that he never dare speak lightly or flippantly. Anything unworthy which he may do reflects on the Sovereign who appointed him. Any lack of dignity, any carelessness in dress or manner, may not be tolerated—he must think always and ever of the reputation of his Royal Master.

The honour and distinctions which that service carries are unlike those of the courts of earth. The most important commission may be entrusted to the humblest servant, and with the commission, the necessary equipment for its execution is supplied. In the case of Christ's Ambassador, the honour is not one of riches and prestige, but of being chosen to convey in Christ's stead an offer of reconciliation to a rebel people. His credentials are the documents he presents, confirming his authority, and his seal of office is the Spirit Whose stamp impresses all he says and does, in fact, all that he is.

The scene changes. That same missionary is in the court of a Chinese inn, talking to a crowd of gaping, inquisitive villagers.

" Is that your Jesus ? " one woman asks when another missionary appears.

" I know Jesus," says another ; " He lives in our village," meaning that one of His disciples lived there.

" Jesus was in our village last autumn," is another man's report, referring to the visit of some itinerant preachers.

The heathen stands looking at a human being who is walking toward him, and actually thinks :

" Here comes Jesus. How will He act ?

" What kind of things does He say ?

" Is He approachable ?

" Is it all right to ask Him into my house ? "

To some, such words may sound blasphemous, to others they appear irreverent, but in no case is blasphemy or irreverence the intention of the speaker. As a matter of fact we have here exactly what the missionary is in an unevangelised land, and, for that matter, what the Christian is in the world.

Christ's Ambassador goes to the uttermost parts of the earth as His representative, the embodiment of His teaching, the demonstrator of His ethics and the upholder of His Name and reputation. It is of no use for him to protest that he is not prepared for such a position, that he never undertook to represent among the heathen the whole character of his Lord. The Christian cannot escape the responsibility of being guardian of his Master's reputation and of His good name, for most of the people who have their eyes on the Christian never turn up the old Book where Christ's portrait is preserved. They just look at His representatives and say : " Christianity is this or that," according to their behaviour.

Herein lies the honour of the missionary's calling. He is a man sent to a far country to speak the name of Jesus to men who have never heard it. It is the greatest honour that can fall to the lot of any man, but whoever accepts it must, with the honour, accept the responsibility of being the interpretation of that new Name wherever he proclaims it.

What manner of men ought ye therefore to be ?

The Postulant—His Call

WHEN Christ's Ambassador revisits his native land he is quickly surrounded by those who are eager to hear his report. As he tells of the joys and sorrows of his service and of the triumphs and failures experienced in the execution of his commission, hearts are stirred and questions pour in on him from eager, enthusiastic men and women.

" Are recruits needed in the service on which you report ? "

" Will the offer of a volunteer be considered ? "

" Will an ordinary man be of use, or does the work require unusual qualifications ? "

" Is it a matter of life-service, or is there a place for short-termers ? "

" You speak of yourself as an Ambassador for Christ. If you were talking of this country's diplomatic service I should understand what you mean and what is the avenue of entrance to the Department. I know that it would necessitate years of hard study and preparation, stiff examinations and, if the effort met with success, toward middle life a possible appointment as ambassador. But the rules of procedure are evidently not the same here. Is every young man who can get himself accepted by a Missionary Society and after comparatively little preparation, sent off to a foreign land, recognised by the Court of Heaven as one of Christ's Ambassadors ? "

" It is an office which no one elects to take for himself; he is called to it by God," replies the missionary, referring to his Book of Instructions. " It is a vocation and therefore can only be entered upon in answer to a call."

" How can I know what constitutes a call ? " is the next eager enquiry. " How does the call reach a man ? When it comes does he know it unmistakably ? Must the call always be a personal one ? Is the general command ' go ' not sufficient in itself ? "

The answer given depends upon the type of missionary who is asked, on his spiritual experience and on his character. In order to give an honest answer each man looks back to the time when he made his own offer of service.

The first sees himself again as a young man of strong executive ability, consumed with a burning desire to put the world right. Just before finishing his college course he attended a great Missionary Meeting at which someone spoke most movingly, and he realised as he never had, the degradation of the heathen world. Compelled by a great urge to help, he warmed as never before to the demands of the brotherhood of man and to the claim of the unfortunate upon the privileged. He had a vision of himself as one called to show to the Indian a Christ who fulfils all the aspirations expressed so inadequately in his own pagan rituals.

To demonstrate in a very practical and concrete manner the meaning of the gospel to the peoples of

India, became the aim of his life. His hopes were realised and he went to that land. On the field his days were filled with actions intended to exemplify the implicates of Christianity, both in the life of the individual and of the community. His answer to the enquiring student is :

" Give yourself as I did and use your life for the uplift of the down-trodden. If you live to the best of your ability, your mission in life will be amply repaid and you will have proved the reality of your vocation."

Another man who was born into the missionary succession and whose very name calls up associations with Africa, when met by the same question looks back to his own farewell meeting, and to the words he spoke there. His family occupied the front row of seats, and he met the look of pride in his mother's eye as he rose to give the testimony for which she so eagerly looked.

" I was brought up in a Christian home by missionary parents," he began, " and while still a child gave my heart to the Lord. During school days I became careless of spiritual matters, but when I was eighteen I attended a boys' camp and there I heard things which made me feel that I too had to be a missionary. I went straight back to tell my parents, confident that they would not grudge me to this service. They have not done so and have given me up willingly."

All this he remembers and reflecting on the service of the past years he thinks : " I really never had to face the difficulties and resistance which is some men's lot." Turning to the enquiring student he says : " All I can say to you is that unless God shuts the door of the mission field to you, it is your duty to go forward. *I* never waited for a special call and why should you ? "

There is always a crowd of questioners pressing round the popular missionary. He may be a doctor whose fame is world-wide for, apart from all other considerations the mission field has been a sphere of big success for him. As a student he was leader of the Christian movement and withal he did so brilliantly at his examinations that when he applied to a Board he was immediately accepted with open arms. There was a lot of talk about him at the time he went out and everyone said : " That fellow would have made his mark anywhere ; he is good at his work and good at games too."

He *has* made his mark and the hospital he built and equipped stands as witness to his capacity, his tenacity and his generosity. He is beloved by the people and his zeal is the motive power of the hospital staff. He gives the young man one straight, serious look.

" A call, did you say ? What constitutes a call ? Look at all that is waiting to be done ; that surely is call enough for us to be up and doing. You have two more years to finish ? Well, don't let it be said that a Christian student comes out with an inferior degree. I hope your appointment is going to be to Melanesia. I should like to have you on my own staff there, later on. You must look for guidance of course, but if you are inclined to apply to the F.F.M.S. (Faith of our Fathers' Missionary Society) I shall put in a claim for you."

It is to be noted that not one of these men has answered the question : " What constitutes a call ? "

The first man's reply leaves it completely out of his reckoning. He has his own view of the contribution entrusted to western civilisation for the uplift of the needy races, and his own sense of responsibility in respect of that contribution, but he has nothing clear to declare about vocational conviction and its grip on the spirit of a man.

The second man was born into a circle where the hope and expectation of the family was that this beloved son should be a missionary. From childhood all the subtle, formative influences suggested the mission field to his mind. It would have taken far more resistance than he was capable of to strike out into some other path, and tell those who loved him so dearly that he had no vocation and no call to either the mission field or the ministry.

The third man found, in the islands of the sea, a scope for his organising capacity which would probably never have been afforded him in England. The hospital of which he is the proud founder, the staff and its numerous activities are his delight. He sees in it an endless vista and opportunity of philanthropic work for Christian young men and women. Only give him enough man-power and there seems no limit to the good he can do.

Yet sometimes the Church welcomes home a man of quite another type. His speaking may be more or less effective, but his impressiveness is not dependent upon eloquence of speech. If he made an appeal for volunteers he would doubtless have abundant response, but he usually seems loath to do so. When the young men get hold of him and ask for help on this problem of recognising a call, he says such stiff things that he leaves his enquirers asking : " Who then can be called ? "

As they question him he looks back to his own conversion, which was for him the passing from death to life and from which he emerged knowing himself to be bought with a price and henceforth not his own. Later on came the almost unbelievable conviction that he was called to witness for Christ in the uttermost parts of the earth. Was it possible and how could he, a man of so few advantages, expect any society to accept him ? Yet, in silence and in solitude he felt the constraint of Christ upon him. He was called by name and not to answer would have been rebellion and disobedience. He faced it out and in one of life's high hours deliberately took a step which committed him to action, safeguarding himself against the attacks of doubt and cowardice.

Immediately, iron doors began to open and this man, who had to rely on the work of his hands for daily bread, found that God had a way to do the impossible. His answer to the young men is uncompromising.

" What constitutes a call ? "

" It is the summons of God to your spirit, for a special and specific service."

" How does the call reach a man ? "

" He will not perceive it through the senses nor reason it through the mind, therefore it is intangible and indefinable."

" When it comes does one know it unmistakably ? "

" It is a breath of God upon the spirit and the spirit of man feels, understands, knows and responds."

" Must the call always be a personal one ? "

26

" Seeing that the service is to be a personal one, the call to it must be personal also."

" Is the general command ' Go ' not sufficient in itself ? "

" For the commission to service, certainly, and a very inclusive command it is—preach the gospel to every creature—but the general call is followed by individual designation. Seeing that the field is the whole world, it is the more needful that each man hear the order which tells him where his own appointed sphere is to be."

" Missionary life, as I hear it presented, has a romantic and appealing side which makes the certainty of the call more difficult to distinguish. When I hear a missionary speak about Africa I think my call is there, yet when I hear one tell of India, or of China, I believe that to be the place to which I should go."

At this, the missionary sat in silence for a moment, seeming loath to put into words what he had in mind. At last he said :

" I fear that the whole issue has been hopelessly confused by the men and women who have gone abroad uncommissioned by their Master. They have increased the staff but weakened the army, and we should have done better without them. In making an appeal they speak of this or of that rather than of the lost condition of those without Christ, and of the compulsion to seek and if possible find them. We should have done better without them.

" The romantic lure ! The picturesque presentation ! Is that what sent Paul of Tarsus, Raymond Lull, Carey, Judson, Henry Martyn, Ragland and Hudson Taylor to foreign lands ? Response to their call meant the loss of everything and was only faced in courageous abandonment of all to the Master they served. We have lowered the threshold. Young men and women even come to me and ask : ' How can I distinguish the call from the romance ? ' To be an Ambassador for Christ would seem to cost them no more than to hold a government appointment in the East. Have none of it. Let your transaction be direct with God. He has a special place for you in His service and if you take time, quiet and silence to find out where that place is, you will certainly discover it.

" A call to the foreign field is absolutely unmistakable to those who have experienced it, and is never to be confused with the easy yield to the line of least resistance which is actual drift and lands a man, who has taken less trouble than a trader does, to investigate and fit himself for his job, on to a foreign shore. There he gradually adapts himself to new conditions and new surroundings and, in order to justify his position, undertakes to preach to the people around him, arrange schools for their children, hospitals for their sick and to organise the religious side of their lives."

Every reader of this book recognises these four types of missionaries. Which of them is right ? They are all men of experience, all held in high esteem, all earnest, all doing a great work. Many voices make jazz, but a shut door and the opening of the disciples' "Book of Instructions," brings order and gives wisdom and discrimination.

The missionary body is now a very large one; some of its members are brilliant, others dull; some are quick, others slow; some are attractive, some are not; some are back-numbers, some are up-to-date; some are stylish, some are dowdy; some are most decidedly "mish," others are more definitely "fash."

The main division, however, is not into any of these classes, and anyone who thinks will acknowledge that there is a stamp upon those who are God-appointed, which is as real, as certain, as unmistakable as are the credentials which an ambassador presents to justify his presence. Christ's Ambassadors carry their insignia; there is just something about them which shows they have had a call—that is all.

" To be or not to be "

IT is somewhat of an anticlimax to emerge from the glow and spiritual fervour of a great experience, as referred to in the last chapter, and to find oneself faced with the printed forms, business-like enquiries and all the mundane details supplied by the Mission Boards to prospective candidates.

With a mind centred on world evangelism it is difficult to face the commonplace enquiries :

" What is your employment ?

How have you spent your time since leaving school ?

Are you liable for any debts ?

Do you have good health ?

Have you read the Bible through ?

Have you any practical knowledge of the following : Carpentry, Cobbling, Cooking, Gardening, Bookkeeping, Teaching, any Musical Instrument, Swimming ? (It is a good thing they include swimming because it is the only thing of the whole lot to which some can say " Yes.")

Are you a total abstainer ?

Do you smoke ? "

There is also a sheet headed : Candidates. Form B. Doctrinal, and this contains a most formidable array of enquiries which it would require a fully trained theologian to answer satisfactorily :

Write below your views on :

" 1. The inspiration of the Scriptures.

2. The Trinity.

3. The fall of man.

4. The atonement.

5. The sacraments."

The most heart-searching question reads :

" Your purpose is to win men to Christ in a heathen land. Have you done so in this country ? "

With this printed paper comes a kind but non-committal letter and a request for a photograph of the applicant.

The applicant sits up till early morning trying to formulate his beliefs on matters of faith and on doctrines which he has always accepted but never before been required to express. The result is a bulgy waste-paper basket and a resolve to try and answer the questions in the words of Holy Scripture or of the Prayer Book, for there he will be on safe ground.

A second evening is spent in turning over these two volumes and selecting suitable phrases from them. The result is very satisfactory, and he produces a set of answers to which it would be impossible to take exception as they contain nothing but texts and the accepted formulæ of the Christian Church.

This further communication is duly acknowledged, but it is rather chilling to find an offer of service for such needy fields met with the suggestion that a considerable period of training may be necessary before being accepted by the Missionary Society.

The deputation who came to College spoke in quite a different tone, and this student is uncomfortably reminded of the recruiting sergeant who catches his man with fine talk and when he has registered and accepted the shilling, runs him to the barrack-yard to learn the goose step.

He had visualised the missionary situation as active warfare and the need as so urgent, that a man with his education would be welcomed and might even be rushed to the front.

He considers the position of a friend of his who, a few months previously, offered himself to a society whose secretary, after the briefest preliminaries, wrote asking him whether, if he were quite sure of his own call, he would be ready to sail in three weeks' time. His passion for souls was such that he telegraphed back " Hallelujah ; ready," cut the remainder of his College course, sailed for Africa and went direct to an unevangelised jungle tribe. A man such as that could have had no dealings with a society which wanted to know all about a side of your life on which you were turning your back for ever.

Yet on reflection, he felt there was something to be said for a Board which requires to know more about the man it accepts and is going to support with money entrusted by their donors. At any rate, the next step for him is to have a photograph taken (they even say it must be postcard size, though what it matters to them whether he is a good-looking fellow or not, he cannot understand). He has filled in the papers, supplied the names of referees and now awaits events.

A week later he gets an invitation to meet the

Board. He does so, and the upshot is disappointing.
He is not quite sure that he showed up as well as he
should have done; the atmosphere was decidedly
difficult. There is no question in his mind about it.
If they turn him down, he is going straight to the
jungle to join old Thompson, whose letters show how
well he is shaping to the work.

He packed up his troubles, along with his pyjamas,
in his old kit-bag, and went off to spend the night
with a man he knew, the kind of man you could not
help trusting. His bed saw very little of him, for
they spent most of the night talking, and next day he
went back to his " digs " a changed man. That
Padre said some straight things, not about the need
of the heathen, but about the need of preparation
before a man should dare to take upon himself the
responsibility of representing Christ to the heathen.
Was he sure of his call ? Was his purpose mature ?
Had he thought that missionary life called for no
preparation, no specialised training ? A few leading
questions showed him that he had no appreciation
of the beliefs which held the minds of the people he
wished to convert, and that he was hopelessly unskilled
in the use of the Scriptures to justify his arguments.

Another interview with the Board resulted in his
being accepted for a training, which would com-
mence as soon as his College course was finished and
probably last for two years. From his new point
of view, it did not now sound an excessive period
of time.

It was a strange community that assembled in that
training college—men drawn from all walks of life.
Educationally he was ahead of most, yet on practical

matters he often felt quite at sea, whereas the man who had had none of his advantages, tackled jobs that baffled him, doing them efficiently and well. The rules and regulations fretted him and he felt it a humiliation to be told at what time to turn out his light and go to bed. The course of study, which had necessarily to be adapted to them all, was given in quite a different way from his College lectures.

He soon saw, however, what a fine lot of men his fellow students were, and at the end of term, when he went to visit the Padre again, he brought a cheering report of his experiences.

" They are awfully decent chaps ; I can see already that many of them will make far better missionaries than ever I shall, but, frankly, I don't see what I'm there to learn. I could get the Bible study for myself out of books, and a few months in the Pentonville Settlement would give much more satisfactory practical work than I am getting. To tell you the honest truth, I have a feeling that the jobs I am given have been prepared with a view to providing a little experience and, incidentally, keeping me busy."

" What are you there for ? " said the Padre. " Well, first of all, to learn how to live with all sorts of men, and you will never learn that with your chums at the Settlement. It isn't so much for you to get to like them, as for it to become possible for them to like you, and that won't take place till some of the rough edges come off you. Your difficulty in bowing to the rules of the establishment shows that you have something to learn in that direction, and I do not see how you will ever bend to the tantalising restrictions of a missionary's life unless, through some irksome curb, you have learnt self-discipline and self-control.

" When you get out to the mission field there may be no one to help you to form good habits of life, early rising, punctuality, methodical study, conscientious preparation and consideration of other people's peculiarities. I know of a missionary so losing his self-control as to strike a native, simply because the man did not pack his cart in the way he liked it done. You think you are too much of a gentleman ever to do a thing like that, but you have never lived in a hot, damp climate, your night's rest destroyed by mosquitoes, malaria in your system, and at the same time having to deal with shifty, lazy, incompetent servants.

" Moreover, if you make the best use of this stage of training, you ought to gain some little skill in handling the weapons of the warfare in which you are to be engaged. One of the chief uses of this period is to give you a chance to put your vocation to the test and judge whether your call to the foreign mission field meets with approval from those who train you or whether they are driven to question its reality.

" There are many other things you have to learn, but they will come later on. Think of this time of preparation as a temporary thing ; if it were prolonged, it would lose all its value, but it will be the making of you if you accept the discipline and learn all that it can teach you."

The Preparation

"A N old-fashioned car, sir," said the garage man as he looked under the bonnet of the Morris Oxford. " But it will do you good service yet, for it belongs to the period before mass production came in, and you will find the benefit of that every time." There is no mass production in the economy of God, and we get the benefit of *that* every time. It marks the difference between man's cleverness and God's supremacy, and makes of every human being an incomparable person. Each is unique and no individual can ever truly be compared with another.

When Job wished to express this fact, he spoke of the seal on the hand of every man,* a seal which we now refer to as his thumb print, and accept as an unmistakable identification. Each man's individuality is as distinct as his thumb mark and the word of warning which might well be written over the door of the Training College is : " Beware of imitation, all ye who enter here." Its intention should be to strengthen unity but not to produce uniformity.

The stamp of personality on the hand has a double use ; it may be fraternal or it may be antagonistic, and it is during the plastic period of youth that the die is cast and the character fixed whether on lines of

* Job xxxvii, 7. He sealeth up the hand of every man. That all men whom he hath made may know it.

generous individuality or of egotistical, assertive individualism.

Each character has its own peculiar snag, therefore resistance to its strong tendencies is essential to its best development. Thus the difficulties of a training period are primarily intended to supply the kind of skilled resistance that the trainer gives to the athlete in order to compel him to draw on fresh reserves of strength. Strength is gained by overcoming obstacles and not by indulging the peculiar bent of personal character, even though this bent be in the nature of a priceless gift. For example, a brainy bookworm should mix with practical men, learn to handle tools and to study the face of nature. When he goes to the East his parishioners will probably be agriculturalists and if he does not know the series of the crops and understand the uses of manure, they will view him as a simpleton, highbrow though he be.

The man who thinks quickly and acts swiftly, requires to learn scrupulous mastery of detail so that when, later on, he is entrusted with a position of authority, he should be found a considerate and reasonable overseer, because he judges accurately how exacting is the demand he makes on his subordinates.

The meticulous man whose contribution of work is painfully small though undoubtedly irreproachable, needs the touch of the goad to force him into the accomplishment of an increased output, even though temporarily his work may suffer in quality. It is as important for him to speed up as it is for the other man to slow down. Therefore the wise trainer harnesses those two men to one job in which both of them will suffer from the other's faults while they are training each other.

The ambitious man, dominated by an urge to excel, is liable to the canker called jealousy, and that dread disease is the cause of so many broken hearts and blighted lives that no leniency can be tolerated in dealing with it.

In money matters, the world is divided into the generously minded and the parsimonious, each of whom needs corrected vision on financial administration. Money is given to man neither to save nor to squander but always and everywhere to be accounted for, both to God and to man, as by a faithful steward whose books are always in order.

Thus every gift, though it will be a valuable asset later on, needs the chisel during training. In years to come when a man has acquired wisdom, understanding, experience, balance, self-control and faithfulness in small things, he will have the qualities which make of his Divinely bestowed peculiarities a unique contribution to the whole body of Christ.

The trainer's job is not an enviable one. Each year he faces a fresh group of students and while each one is as unique as his thumb mark, the trainer, like the thumb print specialist, instinctively places him into his own division and senses the particular line of trouble he may have with him.

" I should say that the main difficulty in producing A1 workers," said one Principal, " comes from the preponderance of those whose piety is in excess of their strength of character."

Intimacy with such students will generally provoke from them the confidence : " I am sorry to find that the atmosphere of the College is not as spiritual as I had hoped. A few of us meet daily for prayer in my room." To the question : " Is there no general D.P.M. at the College ? " the answer is given : " Oh, yes, but we can pray over things more freely where there are only a few of us."

Later on, these people carry this same characteristic on to the mission field and with all their piety, instead of being spiritual rocks, become treacherous creeks where many a good reputation is lost in the quicksand of confidential indiscretions. Under the excuse of praying more freely where only a few meet the law of Christ, which requires that one first speak to one's brother alone, is broken, and the law of loyalty is violated which requires that the junior give his senior credit for best intentions combined with greater knowledge.

They enter every community with a spiritual superiority complex. As in the College the Principal came under criticism, so on the mission field it is the senior missionary who does not measure up to standard. Later on the native clergy and leaders (often men who were established Christians when the young missionary was still an infant) are reported by him to the home constituency as " living on a low spiritual level and sadly in need of revival."

Men of such a character need to acquire, in Training College days, the habit of lonely prayer, the strength to control spiritual gush and confidences, the ambition to attain complete sincerity and incorruptible loyalty.

True, there are Training Colleges where too much that is planned, sought for and imparted to the students, is disregardful of their highest spiritual interests.

There are also some missionary communities where the spiritual tone is flat, where provocation incites to retaliation rather than to good works, and where the spontaneity of the service of first love has given way to the dreary grind of a round of duties fulfilled.

There are undeniably native leaders who, like some of St. Paul's converts, have loved this present world more than they have loved things unseen. Now if the newcomer has eyes to see these things and a heart to feel them, then he has been entrusted with a very delicate piece of work for an inexperienced man, and it behoves him to move carefully, for at that time it is not words, but actions, that count, and in the final issue not even doing, but being.

If he walks humbly with his God he may find later, that, unknown to himself, he was used to remind disheartened leaders of lost ideals, to inspire them to recapture hope and to revive the memory of lapsed pledges and vows. That was true revival, and at the best he will have done his work unconsciously.

Such a fine piece of diplomacy needs the uttermost discretion and tact. Above all it requires that the Ambassador who handles it, preserve silence to everyone except to his King.

" What I fear most," said another Principal, " is the student who adapts himself instinctively to the type he thinks I like—the chameleon man. Of course I see right through it and even sometimes try to stiffen up his resistance by stating the other side of a question, but he veers round in a minute. Shoddy material will not stand strain and I am afraid of that man giving way when everything seems to hang on him. He is the perfect ' yes, yes ' man—a fibreless fellow who will always find a wriggle of escape from the hard things. Now the man whom I find it a joy to train, is the one who refuses to conform to type but who never shirks discipline. Such men always make good."

The Training College offers the last opportunity in many a man's life for him to hear the truth about himself from a person whose desire it is to correct his faults. Therefore, it ought to be a hard time, a time when an experienced man is showing a younger one what he lacks, and that younger one should welcome everything which is going to strengthen, to stiffen, to brace and to toughen him.

This training period is also a time when the contents of the Scriptures should be mastered, not merely read devotionally nor viewed as a text-book for the lecture room, but studied as the volume which makes him wise unto salvation, which equips him for warfare and which will be to him light on every difficult pathway.

The weak side of specialised training is that it affords almost no help in the art of making contacts with all sorts of people. On the contrary it sometimes gives the first touch of " apartness " to a man which, unless deliberately checked, will eventually mark him as one who is segregated from the ordinary paths of everyday life.

The loss, to a missionary, is irreparable. Once he has yielded to it he is probably stamped for life as a man whose profession is preaching and the " professional preacher," stands at a disadvantage both in the East and the West.

Because the tendency to be a man separated from everyday interests can be so easily acquired, it is of primary importance that it be resisted in Training College days and that every effort be made to keep touch with all the normal interests of life.

Think of Jesus Christ, handling a carpenter's tools and representing God to His customers, for well-nigh thirty years.

Any Training College where the habit of prayer is not inculcated is a deception, for now is the opportunity to converse with those to whom prayer is the battlefield where the victories are won, which result on the one hand in personal holiness and on the other in world evangelism. Now must the student learn how to use that most powerful and potent weapon, to learn by experience communion with God, meditation on the things of God, not only how to pray but what to pray for, and how to do God's will and get God's will done on earth as it is done in heaven.

If it be essential to learn to pray, no less urgent is the necessity of coming to understand the meaning of the words " I believe in the Holy Ghost, the Lord and Giver of Life." All the students expect a lonely future where their spiritual life will be sustained by no visible source and it is that Spirit Who will be their final Teacher, Inspirer, Admonisher and Rectifier.

He convicts men of sin, righteousness and judgment. It is by Him that they are born anew. It is He Who leads into all truth and it is only by the power of that Life-giving Spirit that the missionary himself will be a channel of life to others.

Finally, training affords the time when the practice of the presence of God may teach him how every day can be made a holy day, and how even pots and pans may bear the inscription " Holiness to the Lord."

The Objective

SOME years ago a campaign was started in China by
a certain tobacco combine. Its slogan was : " A
cigarette in every Chinese mouth." To this end the
wits, the brains, the money, the energy, the ingenuity
and the drive of all the men engaged on the job, were
concentrated. In the remotest cities of China,
attractive posters appeared, which caught the eye
of every passer-by with pictures of a cockatoo, a
peacock, a pirate, and by the side of each the words :
" Smoke this brand." Sample packets were distri-
buted, merchants were visited everywhere and urged
to stock the goods. The company knew what it
wanted, and set out to get it.

The combine's aim was an easy one to formulate
and the energy with which it was pursued produced
extraordinary results. The cigarette, at that time
almost unknown in inland China, suddenly appeared
everywhere and, having come, it stayed. The popu-
lace had acquired the " cigarette habit." Half the
success of the enterprise was due to the fact that there
was no ambiguity as to objective, and the endeavour
was of a kind to capture public attention immediately
and to yield quick results.

Unlike the merchant, many a missionary has started

43

out with but the most nebulous idea as to his purpose. Broadly speaking, the answers received to the enquiry : " What is your objective in becoming a missionary ? " take some of the following forms :

1. I am out here to teach the true brotherhood of man.
2. My aim is that the African might be reconciled to God.
3. To share my good things with a less favoured race.
4. My objective is to make my fullest contribution to the uplift of a heathen people.
5. I am out here for the salvation of souls.
6. To show the people a Christ who is the fulfilment of the best in their own religion.
7. What am I here for ?   To preach the Gospel.
8. To seek the salvation of souls in China.
9. That the Lord Jesus may see of the travail of His soul in me, in others, and be satisfied.

The clear wording of one's objective is not an easy matter, but a man might well be called a fool who, starting out on a life career for which he gave up everything, was unable to produce a clear statement as to why he was doing it.

To Christ's Ambassador there is no ambiguous objective ; he is told to preach, to teach, and to beseech men in Christ's stead to be reconciled to God.   He has been sent where warfare is active between his King and the usurper who is called " prince of this world."   He is authorised to declare the freedom of all captives who turn from the power of Satan to

44

God, to declare the remission of sins, to hasten the coming of Christ's Kingdom and the accomplishment of His will on earth.

Preaching, teaching and baptising are but means to this end, and as he preaches, teaches and baptises, many things will incidentally happen : superstitions will lose their power, a new standard of morality will appear, the value of life will be recognised, slavery will go, the sick and the infirm will be cared for, woman will take her rightful place in society, child-life will assume a new importance and even illiteracy will vanish.

Put the objective right and all these things will happen in due order, but make of any one of them an objective and no radical reform will take place. Civilisation may appear, but " Civilisation drives away the tiger and breeds the fox."

The thinking out of call, commission and objective cannot be done in a crowd. Paul was one of the best equipped men of his age, and there was no doubt about his conversion, yet he speaks of an experience, apart from these things, which might well have a place in everyone's life : " I went into Arabia."

He is silent as to what took place there, but it put him into a certain relationship with Christ and gave him an understanding of his commission, which freed him of any further need to confer with flesh and blood, and rectified his whole outlook on life as is evidenced by the unique quality of his missionary work. Henceforth he knew what he had to do, and he did it. He knew what he had to say, and he said it. In a word, he knew, and there only remained obedience.

Geographically a man may be far removed from Arabia or from any other desert, but it is probably possible for him to get alone for a few days, in a quiet place ; most people can do so if they care enough. It is the lack of that experience which accounts for so much that is incomplete, undisciplined, unripe and immature among missionaries.

There is a certain spiritual experience which is best expressed by those words : " I went into Arabia," which everyone should secure before embarking on a life work. What happens there is not to be the subject of the farewell address, for to every disciple the command is sometimes given, though it would seem as if some never heard it : " Seal up the things which thou hast heard."

The Protestant Church will arrange endless Conventions, meetings, week-ends and house-parties with unlimited opportunity for a few to talk and a number to listen, but to its loss, it stands aloof from encouraging periods of quiet, solitude, silence, and the detachment which affords opportunity for hearing God speak. It is in gatherings of Christian people, in Church services, in listening to addresses, in sharing testimony or in united intercessions that a man receives deep impressions, but his individual commission is a tremendous personal transaction and demands silence. If the Church does not help us in this matter, then we must arrange for ourselves.

The occasion is urgent, for to start on a missionary career without giving time enough to hear what the Lord has to say to one, is impudent self-sufficiency and entails irreparable loss. It may be compared with an Ambassador leaving for a foreign appointment and neglecting the opportunity of receiving his letters of introduction and his instructions direct from his King.

During retreat all noise, interruptions, letters and newspapers, and the disturbing detail of everyday life should be shunned, for it is essential to give oneself up to the business in hand. It is sensible to take all the sleep required and long walks will probably help. Hours alone in a field, out of the sight of man, certainly will. It should be borne in mind that the object of this retreat is not to get subjects for sermons, addresses, nor Bible readings for future use. This time *you* are the person concerned and no one else, and you are here for a personal audience.

Let no envoy start out under instructions to teach and preach " all these things " without asking to be told what is meant by the words " all things," for it is an awful responsibility to shake beliefs that have held any man's soul for a lifetime, and no one should do it lightly or irresponsibly. In fact, no one is justified in doing it at all, unless he be personally and profoundly convinced that what he offers is Truth and Life. Honesty should be the basis of every missionary's mental equipment.

Loneliness is a test, and self-examination in solitude lacks the excitement of the revival meeting, but it also avoids the desolation of its subsequent reaction. It does not even offer the subtle relief of confession to a human being. Performed in simplicity it brings the sinner directly before the Judge, and there is no outcome from that interview other than rectification and reformation, along with the renewed and deepened love which results from full and free forgiveness.

Many forms of self-examination will suggest themselves, and each one has its value, but it is a sharp pull up even to ask oneself in solitude : " Is there any one single thing in which I am stricter with myself at this hour, than I was twelve months ago, or are all the ropes just a little slacker ? "

Adjustment A

THE farewell meeting and the send-off are like a great wave which carries the skiff over the coral reef but bears the craft from the safe waters of harbour into the open sea. The veteran knows it, the young recruit seldom realises it. He is probably suffering from a great illusion partly due to the play of limelight which has recently been focussed on him, both on platforms and in circles where the missionary enjoys far more prestige than he deserves.

Perhaps it was something to do with the unaccustomed glare, which dazzled his eyes and deluded his very mind, but he has certainly come to feel that when he lands on a foreign shore, it will be as a very different man from the fellow he has hitherto known himself to be.

He feels that his new environment will help him, being quite different from the college or the business house, with their manifold distractions, and the not thoroughly congenial home atmosphere in which he vaguely realises that he has been a bit of a problem. On the mission field, witness for Christ is going to be much easier. It will be the one and only business of his life and there will be no conflicting claims to interfere. Every man must have a profession, and *his* chosen profession is that of soul-winning—a glorious calling. He feels there will be safety in whole-hearted devotion and he is determined that other things shall not be allowed to divert his attention from the main business.

Meanwhile the novel experiences of his first sea journey are, for the time being, as much as he can handle. Fellow passengers have recognised the group of youngsters as a band of incipient missionaries and, as such, view them askance and from afar. This then is the first lesson in the new life—how to bear himself as one who is unassuming yet dignified, approachable yet not inclined to familiarity, gay yet not light, serious yet not self-important.

To learn how to take part in all that is good and pure, but silently to rebuke all that is otherwise. To know how to associate with all sorts and conditions of men without losing stability. To know how to carry out the instruction which Paul the aged gave to young Timothy—" Let no man despise thy youth." These are lessons of major importance to the man who would be an Ambassador, for the way in which he masters them will influence the nature of his future service and the character of work which will be entrusted to him.

The impression produced by the first sight of an Eastern people is difficult for the callow missionary to formulate. He steps on shore, and immediately a swarm of black, brown or yellow-skinned men, circle round this pink specimen, who has somehow become a centre of activity, much as a fragment of extraneous matter sets an ant-hill in agitation. He looks at them and tries to realise that these are the heathen, who, in their blindness, bow down to wood and stone, but here they are, quite jolly and happy and handling the ordinary business of life uncommonly well.

The wharf is lined with grinning children demanding to make sensational dives for coins, coolie life is a revelation of man power and each unit is as physically able for his job as a thoroughbred animal, the result of generations of specialised training. One thing, however, rather horrifies him, that is how easily quarrels break out and when they do so, the blaze of fierce elemental passions which they release is terrifying. He saw several rickshaw men competing for a fare, and one man who failed to get it, was left bleeding by the roadside because he was physically inferior to the others.

Days go by and on the whole, the more he sees of the native, the better he likes him. He seems to be a happy, irresponsible creature who lives a sunshine life, works, eats, sleeps and asks for nothing more. Once, however, he was awakened at midnight by the distant sound of tom-toms and the lilt of a quavering falsetto voice. There was something in the weird rhythm which recalled things he had heard from missionaries or read in their books, and he felt the presence of something evil. His spirit recognised in that sound a devilish thing, stronger than himself, and fear roused him so effectively that for the first time in that land, he arose, drew his sword, and knelt to pray. Of course he had taken part daily in public and private intercession, but this was different. He was genuinely frightened and called out : " Lord, save me."

As was his send-off from the homeland, so is his

reception on the other shore, where kind, thoughtful, considerate people meet him, put his luggage through the Customs and smooth the initial difficulties from his path. A few days later, a railway ticket is bought for him and he is placed in a very comfortable train along with a well-packed food basket. The journey is very enjoyable, and twenty-four hours later, the train draws up at a station where a seething mob of strange people move up and down, shouting, gesticulating, fighting, pushing, but where he sees a Britisher making his way through the crowd to get at him.

With relief he finds himself once more in competent hands, he steps into a car and an hour later has reached the house which will be his home for the next twelve months. Seated in a cool, airy room, with electric fans whirring, a dark-faced servant in spotless white brings him an iced drink, and murmurs a respectful greeting. Everyone is superlatively kind, and when he has walked in the garden, among the luxuriant flowers, then been left alone in his own rooms, he looks around and decides that life is certainly going to be easier here than it was at home where things were often pretty strenuous.

In a few weeks' time the heat, the unusual food and the heavy perfumes begin to tell upon him. Then comes a monsoon which compels a change of clothes four times a day and every garment drops with a thud on the floor so heavy is it with perspiration. Mosquitoes are legion and so hungry! His hand sticks to the page of his study book and when he tries to lay down his pen, it clings to his fingers. He asks himself how he is ever going to work in an exhausting climate like this. There is no snap, no brace, no toughening of his physical frame, and the old love of ease is back on him.

What guarantee had he to count upon a radical change in his character when he reached a foreign shore? The difficult home people and neighbours are certainly much farther away, but he is going to live with others who may be even less congenial, and he will certainly be thrown into a proximity with them such as he has never known before. In his own land, he was able to move about with freedom, but here, life will be more circumscribed and he will soon find that the compound walls shut him in to his difficulties and that there is no escape from them.

He has never reckoned with the fact that, from the moment of his appointment, he, as Christ's Ambassador, was a marked man. Every characteristic, every talent, the nature of his pleasures, indulgences, failings, his peculiar idiosyncrasies and besetting sins were mercilessly noted by the enemy, for exploitation. He is going to be made the target of a most subtle and crafty attack, whose director is the father of lies. No trouble will be spared to counter or maim him. If he can only be deflected in these early days, one hair's breadth from the straight course, a few years will take him wide of the goal; if he can now be effectively dealt with, he may later on be left alone to pursue his devious course unmolested.

Adjustment B

THE missionary's responsible life begins from the day when he can talk to be understood and so understand that he can be talked to. He is now no longer a new arrival, to be handled by well-meaning seniors; he can manage for himself and starts his career in earnest.

From this moment he begins to establish relationships, the character of which will probably persist all through his missionary life, and his native *entourage* quickly begins to classify him according to his natural genus. In public they are prepared to call him "Bishop," "Reverend," "Pastor," "Sahib," "Teacher," or, indeed, by any other "big name" that his missionary society ordains, but in private they reserve to themselves the right to fit him with a "small name," generally of rare accuracy, for it is the result of keen observation. By this he is known everywhere and to every native, on every occasion, except officially.

In China, if he be arrogant, he may be called "high-nose"; if he be swift in decision, he may be termed "the wind"; a man of outstanding ability is often known as "the tiger," and it takes a surprisingly short time for a native community to sum up a man's outstanding characteristics and unanimously stamp him with a nickname.

With each fresh arrival a word travels through the *bazar* : " Quick-tempered ; don't rouse him," or " There is nothing in him to rouse." " Boasts the wisdom of heaven, but has none of this world's ; beware of his advice." " He loves ' in the Lord ' " (that is, without spontaneous affection). " Good head for business ; better merchant than priest." For super-praise, the brief word, " Sincere man," suffices.

Most Orientals reserve their greatest admiration for a certain jade-like quality of character. The man who is serene at all times, controlled both in joy and sorrow, and insulated from the turmoil of life, fascinates the Buddhist whose ideal is to pass through this world utterly unmoved by its passions, distresses, or pleasures, and take as straight a course as possible toward the oblivion of Nirvana. But the missionary is not there to court the admiration of the native. He is there to make the unique contribution which is his alone to make toward the upbuilding of the Church.

Yet he may be full of good intentions and well furnished unto every good work, but for lack of some initial adjustment to the delicacies of racial complexities, his intentions will never come to fruition nor his good works meet with appreciation. The fact is that in order to make contribution effective, he must come to know his people and find a means of establishing a way of communication with them by means of which they can understand one another. He will only do this if he has Ezekiel's patience and will sit for seven days " where they sat " before he begins to deliver the Word of the Lord to them.

The only basis of satisfactory relationship in life is sincerity, expressing itself in the mutual confidence which draws out each man's personal contribution and unites various personalities into what is best spoken of as a team, that is, sharing of enthusiasms, interests and purposes along with the sinking of individual ambitions and any thoughts of personal aggrandisement. Team work involves confidence, but not necessarily confidences.

The junior missionary is now at one of the crises of his life. He is very liable to make mistakes which he will forget, but which will never be forgotten by others and he needs extreme wariness. He knows enough of the language to express himself, but has not yet complete understanding of the full bearing of the phrases he uses. Eastern languages are highly idiomatic, and in all such languages one may easily say things one never intended to say.

Although he now understands with delightful ease when people speak directly to him, yet he does not catch the point when they turn round and speak to each other. The reason for this is that what the native wishes him to understand is couched in " compound talk," what he says to his own compatriot is in the *patois* of the country, and not until the missionary can freely understand *that* talk, does he come at the thought behind the words.

Simultaneous with the laborious process of mastering the subtleties of the language, is the harder task of exploring the involutions of an oriental mind, and it is providentially appointed that language is acquired

but slowly. Were the gift of tongues so freely imparted that the newcomer could express himself
easily from the beginning, his loss would far exceed
his gain. Exuberances, enthusiasms and effusiveness
are things to hold in check until he so handle the
language that he knows exactly what its idiom
conveys.

An Easterner will never misunderstand dignity
and reserve, but he will certainly misunderstand a
relationship from which they are absent. It takes
years of experience to appreciate the Eastern method
of procedure—the roundabout way of coming to
the point, the introduction of a middle-man on every
occasion to act as witness and go-between in each
transaction so that not even a cook can be engaged or
dismissed without his assistance.

A problem which requires still more wisdom is that
of appreciating the different attitude toward truth in
East and West, and the indulgent view taken of
actions which rouse the missionary's indignation but
leave the oriental conscience quite undisturbed. The
missionary slowly perceives that the people regard
anger, impatience and even uncompromising justice,
as faults which are more serious defects of character
than a little immorality, dishonesty and untruth,
chiefly because they cause so much more trouble.

He must learn to view his own racial, natural and
personal defects with as much severity as he applies
to judgment of the native. He must be easy-
going to neither. The best stepping-stones through
this morass are spiritual comradeship, sharing of
work and of the hardships inherent to that work.

When two men tramp the roads on an evangelistic

effort, reading the Bible together, praying together, and preaching together, relationships simply, naturally and normally right themselves. In Bible study the missionary will probably be teacher, in prayer both are equal—redeemed sinners kneeling before " Our Father " ; in preaching, conversation and contacts, the missionary is learner. As regards hardships, they fall much heavier on the Westerner, for the other man has never known a higher standard of life, and the hospitality they receive as they go, is, to him, luxury.

On such occasions the missionary will probably be faced with one of those subtle dalliances with truth, which are so baffling. The Christian man, his companion, constantly suggests that " The Reverend " is enduring degrees of hardship from which he really ought to find an escape by living in a house, or hiring a man to carry his pack, by bringing foreign stores or even by sitting at home during the extreme heat, the extreme cold, the rainy season and the period known as " excited insects."

The only way which leads to mutual respect is for the young man to refuse to see any hardship in the job at all. When the sympathetic commiserators come round saying : " What difficulties you have encountered on this journey ! What bitterness you have endured ! What hardship you have met ! " he must refuse to hear a word of it. When his hostess says : " You have never eaten such poor food before," the only answer he can make is : " Madame, your food is excellent ; your flour is of the finest and your skill in handling the materials surpasses that of my own mother."

Adjustment B

Truth generally consists in the use of such idiom as represents facts to the mind of the hearer, and this sentiment, from the lips of a Westerner, merely conveys to his kind hostess that he recognises the trouble that has been taken on his behalf and appreciates her care for him.

The adjustment of these first years is not only that of the physical being, to climate, food, travel and general conditions, but that of the mind to other atavisms and racial divergencies of thought.

That adjustment must be made under the guidance of the Holy Spirit and in the fire of Divine love, so that the elements may be fused and welded to a perfect amalgam. Moreover, it must be effected promptly as it will probably be made now or never.

Let it be now !

Cyril Simpkins Soliloquises

CYRIL SIMPKINS was in a reflective mood. The mail brought him a copy of his favourite weekly and he looked at once at his pet column which was headed " Answers to Miscellaneous Questions." He often marvelled at the versatility of the man who conducted this " Enquire within " and who had a ready answer for every poser. He never seemed to reach the point when he had to say : " I don't know " or " There is no answer to this question."

Cyril had an immediate problem and he wondered how the Rev. Thomas Nowall would deal with it. It was " How can one young missionary fulfil the command which bids him be all things to all men ? " At home, life had seemed comparatively simple. There he was not faced with such manifold relationships as make a special demand upon him out here. It is now three years since he sailed from England and he is half-way toward his first furlough. He would have liked to have started on that furlough with the happy feeling that he had measured up. He enumerates the principal claims made on his personality and to each of these he desires to respond adequately.

1. He is paying guest in the household of a mission-

ary couple, the Rev. B. and Mrs. Makeover. This relationship requires tact.

2. He is " Uncle Cyril " to the Makeover children. This demands long-suffering.

3. He is master to his servant, and this relationship, he has already discovered, needs wisdom.

4. He is member of the mission station staff. This requires of him a competent contribution in a spirit of diffident dignity.

5. He is one of a team, and must take an even share in every effort.

6. He is head of a department. This demands zeal, diligence and consideration.

7. He is guest of the native Church, and so far fails to see what is required of him as such.

Cyril is a methodical worker and as he meditates he reaches for a pencil and a piece of paper. As he thinks, he draws. He visualises these varied relationships as the spokes of a wheel of which he himself is

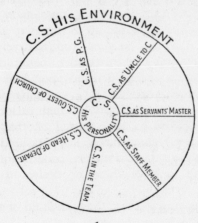

hub and his little world the rim. Each spoke represents an avenue of contact with that world.

Cyril looks at his tidy work, quite pleased with the effect, and murmurs :

" Yes, that's it. Let me now think out how I measure up to these claims."

1. *Cyril as Paying Guest*

I always hated them. I remember the year when Father had money difficulties and Mother said it might help if we took a couple of boarders ; how we all rose up and yelled : " Oh, Mother, anything but P.G.s ! " We felt we would rather go short of a lot of things than have an everlasting stranger among us. Now the tables are turned and I am the P.G. How am I behaving myself in that capacity ?

Food. The standard of this house is medium. Mrs. Makeover is not a good manager and meals are often haphazard. When the bread was sour and the mince was too salt I did not hide my annoyance. She is always changing her cook and in the gaps has to produce meals herself. Now I come to think of it, why should Mrs. Makeover wait on Cyril Simpkins ? When I became a missionary did I really expect to be served or to serve ? Is it possible that I have sunk so low as to grumble at the food which my hostess puts on her table ?

Punctuality. Really Mrs. M. has been pretty patient with me, for I'm generally late. My inconsiderateness in this matter has led to a lot of friction and unpleasantness. This won't do.

Tidiness. I think I have measured up here, though it hasn't been easy in this untidy house.

General considerations. Room for improvement. Must think out ways of helping. Might have done a bit more for their boy when he was home from school. It must be jolly awkward for them to have me always in the house. This wretched courtyard plan! I can't help overhearing a great deal of what they say to one another. I must cultivate the quality of discretion.

I put my foot in it once when I wrote home about James going to Branckton Hill School. They talked it out at table and never said it was private, but when it came out that I had spread the news, it was decidedly awkward. Now I come to think of it, it was awfully stupid of me not to realise that unless they can trust me *never* to report their affairs, their home life is just spoilt by my presence in the house. I *must* learn to mind my own business, hold my tongue, and cultivate that blind spot in my eye.

The worst of it is, people *will* ask indiscreet questions—things they would never ask me about my own family. There must be a reticence about me which puts a stop to it and shows everyone that for the time being we are like one family and we stand by each other. By the kindness of the Makeovers I am admitted to a footing of extraordinary intimacy and such intimacy demands absolute loyalty.

Memo : I must learn never to ask questions which might put another fellow, situated as I am, in the same difficulty.

Query : What kind of temperament makes an ideal P.G. ? He must not be moody or uncertain, he must not be touchy, he must not be fiery. To make everyone happy, he should have a sunny temperament ;

sorry I haven't got it!   In correcting myself I must not aim at sunniness, as I should only succeed in being bright, like good old Brasso, who makes you feel that he has rubbed himself up before breakfast when he comes down with a grinning face and shoots nippy, optimistic sentences at you.   What I must aim at, is steadiness and reliability.

2. *Cyril as uncle to the kiddies*

I was reading up an old note-book last night and I found this warning from a veteran : " Your senior missionary may be an A1 man but he may have a C3 wife, or he may be a B2 man with an A1 wife. Even if they are both Class A people, they may have XYZ children."   It has got to be faced out that the kiddies here, converge toward the end of the alphabet. What child would not in this climate and, after all, if I had taken up children's work as I once thought of doing, I should have met with lots that were worse and viewed it as my mission in life to try and help them to be better.

Memo : This matter to be thought out in detail. How about getting a few games from home ?   The poor Makeovers would never think of it.

3. *Cyril as master of a servant*

I have never approved of the haughty relationships which I consider exist between missionaries and their servants.   This way, for example, of never saying " thank you," but just taking their service for granted, and I thought it showed great lack of consideration to make a cast-iron rule about not paying wages in advance.

I certainly had a difficult time with my last man ; he left me ten days ago and over such a trifle. I lost my luminous match box and, when I asked him if he had seen it, he imagined that I accused him of stealing, flew into a terrific rage and walked out of the house. I found the match box after all, so he hadn't taken it. Apparently my question was too abrupt and I upset him.

I feel I made a failure in my relationship with that man, though I did try to help him. Mr. Makeover warned me about being too intimate with him, but of course, I could not expect him to share his family affairs with me unless I spoke friendlily to him and a little about my own background seemed the only way to establish contact. It did not work. He even went away and told someone that my father made a living by standing at the roadside with a tray of toffee hung round his neck. That was just because I gave him a few sweets and told him they were made in my father's factory.

I shall go more slowly with this new man. When he showed me his torn sleeve and asked if I had any bits to patch it with, I said " no." Perhaps Makeover is right and it is better to command respect than to provoke intimacies.

4. *Cyril as member of the Mission Station staff*

It is true I am a junior, but I have a contribution to make and while others have the pull over me in knowledge of this country, I certainly have the pull over them in a more up-to-date training. We are not exactly a smooth-running company. Our upbringing has been too different. It reminds me of the old bus at the training home, with its grinding gears. Each time we discuss, there is apt to be a crash and a jar. We are getting to be so conscious of friction that we do not talk things out freely together. We shall have to adjust the engine and I must not get out of my part in doing that. There is only one way that I can see. I will go over to the other compound to-morrow and get an hour's talk with H. I am afraid I hurt his feelings at the last staff meeting and it's up to me to apologise before things go any further.

5. *Cyril as head of a department*

It was a sheer bit of luck that I was put into this post when Jones smashed up and had to go home. Now I have the hospital in my own hands for a year, and there are going to be some changes. I haven't been going about with my eyes shut since I came, and I see plenty of room for improvement all round. I *must* get my department up to standard, whatever it costs. I can't think how Jones put up with the slack, semi-Eastern way in which the thing is run. The natives tell me that I shall get no patients if I refuse to have their relatives squatting on the premises. Well, we shall see. Jones's point of view was evangelism before everything and there is no denying that he got some keen men round him. I see they don't like my new proposal. I am certainly head but I can only work through them and if I don't carry them with me we shall be on the rocks.

I feel that I am up against a real difficulty and what shall I have gained if I get my own way and antagonise my assistants?

The Apostle Paul wrote some great instructions about those who were masters and those who were under them, doing God's will from the heart, in mutual confidence. Perhaps if I went more slowly I should secure the co-operation of the whole hospital staff, and incidentally it would give me time to write home to Jones and ask his advice also. It is not very courteous never to mention the changes to him until they are accomplished. *I* should not like it, and if I love my neighbour as myself it means treating other people as I like others to treat me.

6. *Cyril as member of a team*

I wrote this down because there is so much talk nowadays about team work, and there is something very pleasant about the thought it suggests. Here am I, a Britisher on Asian soil, among an Asian people. Are they and I called to be fellow-members of a team which has to train until all have learned to co-operate in such a way that each man knows perfectly how to play the game for the honour of his side and not for himself? From what I've seen of Eastern boys, I think it would be the making of them to get this into their minds. Unfortunately the missionaries in this community are such a set of individualists. One talks exclusively about his school, while the very word " school " is anathema to Hodge, our village-work crank. I myself know how doctoring bodies can absorb your time and interest, till you talk of nothing else.

Now Mr. Brand, who belongs to the mission known as the " One and Onlies," has no use for anything but revival meetings, and as soon as a man

is converted he begins to talk about reviving him.
The bother is that each one of these individualists
has succeeded in making the native who works with
him two-fold more the child of individualism than
he is himself. How can such a heterogeneous group
ever form a team? I don't know. I can't change
them, but I must beware of being such an individualist
myself that *I* become impossible as member of a
team.

7. *Cyril as guest of the native Church*

A strange title by which to call a missionary. I
should never have thought of it, but last week I
heard one of the native clergy speak of Makeover
as " guest of the native Church." I suppose he calls
us all guests. What does he mean by that? Of
course I am only a lay member of the staff, but when
I was at College it was touch and go if I should take
Orders. If I were a clergyman would they still call
me a guest? I thought I came here as a pillar of the
Church, not a guest. I must think this out and talk
it over with the right people. I'd like to know
what that canny Elder thinks about it. I must not
let my ideas on Church administration crystallise.
Keep fluid, Cyril! I must re-read the Acts of the
Apostles with this in mind.

Cyril Simpkins put out his hand for the slight
volume of Weymouth's translation of the New
Testament, and turned over the leaves for a few
moments. Something caught his eye and he read:

" Then Barnabas paid a visit to Tarsus to try and
find Saul. He succeeded, and brought him to
Antioch; and for a whole year they were the guests

of the Church, and taught a large number of people."*

"Hullo," he exclaimed, "I never knew before that those very words were in the Bible. That settles it."

He took up his pen again and wrote : " Well, if I have to accept the position of guest, it will entail on me a most exacting loyalty in all I say, write or even think about my host.   In this mission people seem to regard themselves as school masters to send in candid reports on the character and doings of the native Church members to people at home, who, in turn, view themselves as entitled to know everything about them.   They say it helps them to pray, but if I wrote home asking prayer for Fleming's temper and Farrar's jealousy, I should hear of it.   I wish I had that last circular back in my hands ; I would strike out a few personal bits, because they really do sound rather caddish when viewed as having been written by a guest, about his host."

Cyril looked back at his diagram and murmured : " Seven spokes, seven relationships. The perfect number, requiring the perfect man to meet them and for such service as this, who is competent ?   Just one thing : the wheel jars unless well oiled, and it is oiled at the hub. The hub, for me, is Cyril Simpkins himself."

* Acts xi, 25, 26.

Heathendom—What it really is

At no time does a man need to be more sure of his commission and more clear on his objective, than at the hour when necessary adjustments are taking place. He should remind himself that the Ambassador uses every form of courtesy among the people to whom his appointment takes him, speaking their language, and adapting himself to their culture and manner of life, yet without yielding one inch on any point where the interests of his King are involved. He is the King's representative, and loyalty to his Royal Master is his first consideration.

If his own objective has been, and is, direct, he will instantly be on the alert when worldly people and even, possibly, some who profess Christianity, state the view that every nation must have its own method of expression in things religious. Why interfere? The black stone of the primitive tribe, the grotesque idol, the tablet or the little placid gilded figure of Buddha, appear to them as merely expressing man's need of a focus-point of worship. Each race is at a different point of the road, but all will come to God—by a more circuitous route, certainly, but they will end there.

He may be amazed to find that some missionaries are even prepared to welcome a gesture of patronage from Eastern cults, by which Jesus is offered a place in their Pantheon, and honoured as " the great teacher of the West," his appointed niche being one of equality with Buddha, Confucius and Mohammed, all of whom are spoken of as " light-bearers " in varying degrees. The quality of homage offered to humanity's " Elder Brother," is so subtly and delicately expressed, that while his spirit scents danger, his mind inclines to admit the advantage of this friendly advance, and instinctively gives it a certain consideration.

This man has already had opportunity of seeing how avenues of approach, both to native heathen and compatriot pagans, have been closed by fanaticism without love, and attack without reason. He feels that he cannot let himself be coerced by ruthless enthusiasts into a " bull in the china shop " attitude, which he feels to be un-Christlike, but still less can he consider any toning down of the message which he came across the world, at great cost, to deliver.

" God so loved the world, that He gave His only begotten Son, that whosoever believeth in Him should not perish but have everlasting life."

" I am the way, the truth, and the life : No man cometh unto the Father but by Me."

" In none other is there salvation : for neither is there any other name under heaven that is given among men wherein we must be saved."

" The whole world lies in the power of the evil one."

" The god of this world hath blinded the minds of them which believe not, lest the light of the glorious gospel of Christ . . . should shine upon them."

"For there is but one God, and one mediator, between God and men, the man Christ Jesus, who gave Himself a ransom for all men, to be testified in due time. And of this testimony I was appointed herald and apostle."

These are the exclusive terms of his commission, and he has no authority to alter them.

He meets, in turn, some of the lovable people who are so eclectic, and some of the much less lovable ones who are so impeccably sound in dogma, and so unapproachable on any matter where even a small difference of theological term is in question. The one is conspicuous by the faultlessness of his doctrine, the other by his generosity and love, but to neither of them can he turn in this difficulty. Who, then, can help him?

Thank God there is one man in the community who is a rock—just that. Whether it be doubts, questions, failures, or problems of any kind, one can talk it out with him, and depend on him never to break confidence. When consulted by anyone in trouble, he turns on him a look so interested, so honest, so thoughtful and so self-forgetful, that his visitor quite naturally opens up his whole heart and thought to him. This man has a spacious mental guest-room, to which anyone in distress has access, and where he roams at large and is never hurried. He never pretends to have reached a conclusion unless he has really done so, he always welcomes a contribution of thought on any subject, and he never, never shuts up the seeker by turning him down with a text of Scripture or with a commonplace sentiment.

To him the perplexed missionary turned, confident of a patient hearing, and of not being interrupted. While the younger man talked, the elder listened.

" My dear fellow," he said at last, " the enemy is kicking up dust in order to confuse you. It is part of his strategy ; anything to divert you from the main issue. You are here with a message of reconciliation and of liberty to the captives, toward whom you must feel nothing but love, compassion and pity. On the other hand, you must not tolerate the slightest degree of compromise with the one who has captured them, for he is the arch-enemy of your King." Then turning to his files he drew out a pile of MSS.

" I have given a great deal of thought to the subject of heathendom, what it is, and what it is not," he said. " Take these notes and look them through—they may help you."

While the elder man went off to his business, the younger sat and read :

" The study of Eastern religions has often led to the question whether they are not the normal and best expression of the people who follow them. It can be argued that Confucianism and Buddhism are better suited to the Chinese mind than Christianity, and that the Hindu and Brahmin find a satisfaction in their own rites and ceremonies which Christianity would never give them.

" Tribal customs, even slavery and the segregation of woman, are part of the social organisation of remote peoples, and the break-up of that organisation, which becomes essential directly Christianity enters the field, causes temporary chaos and makes the critic of missions deplore interference which brings in its

73

train a sword, while professing to be the vanguard of the army of the Prince of peace.

" On the other hand the world of art finds among the gorgeous temples of India, the geisha girls of Japan, the theatrical performances in old China, a charming touch of local colour, and feels they must be rescued from the violent hands of the iconoclast. While there is general sympathy with the philanthropist, who carefully and gradually helps to raise the pagan, it is only on condition that in helping the oppressed he spare the artistic decorations of the heathen rites and stop short of spoiling the pleasure of the entertainment.

" Many missionaries confine their efforts to social service, and to the amelioration of low conditions, hoping that by gradual raising of the standard of life, a new order may emerge that will see in Christianity the only religion possible to modern civilisation.

" All these evade a direct clash with the Satanic forces and simply do not understand the meaning of the words : ' Ours is not a conflict with mere flesh and blood, but with the despotisms, the empires, the forces that control and govern this dark world—the spiritual hosts of evil arrayed against us in the heavenly warfare.'

" Heathendom is not a low social condition, it is not poverty, it is not bad customs, it is not even an inferior code of morals. Heathendom is the condition of men and women whose worship is not directed toward God, but toward Satan, whose minds Satan darkens, lest the light of the glorious Gospel of the blessed God should shine upon them. Their development is arrested, and their souls entombed.

" They are supplied with a symbol of worship, but behind the little black stone is the great spirit of fear, gripping the heart of the man who pours oil upon it. Behind the hideous idol lurks the being to whom idol-worship is directed, and behind the contemplative Buddha presides the prince, whose one and only aim is to divert homage from Him Who alone is entitled to receive it, God the Father Almighty, Maker of heaven and earth.

" God is Father of Light, and Satan is father of lies. God is the Giver of life, and Satan a murderer from the beginning. The children of light move onwards on a pathway of increasing light, but the children of darkness become ever more deeply involved in a labyrinthine tangle of illusion.

" Of this the heathen world supplies innumerable illustrations. Here is a shrewd merchant, whose business ability is a byword with his fellows. When the sun is setting, he starts off to the temple, basket on arm, to burn gilt paper, folded like money, for his dead mother's use in the land of shadows. He should have buried silver money with her, but paper saves expense, and is accepted as currency in business dealings with demons. The priests say that he can help his mother to more speedy re-incarnation, if he supply her with enough money to tip the demons when she crosses the bridges of the courts of hell. Those demons have no mercy, but like the men of the world which he knows, they are ready to do anything for gold.

" The beautiful little Indian bride enters her new home amid bowers of flowers, gorgeous and profuse. Everyone is garlanded, and everyone is gay, but with-

75

in a week she is a widow, and the gods have declared her to be an accursed thing. She is unwanted, feared, hated, an object of ill-omen, and her husband's death must be due to her sin. With shaven head, and dressed in the coarsest garments, she shrinks away, for the very sight of her may bring misfortune, and though she be spared suttee, her life from henceforth is but a living death.

" The Chief of an African tribe has died. His sun must sink in red. *Mpaki* is the dread term for the institution which demands living sacrifices at his funeral.

" The procession is in train for a start, when out spring lynx-eyed negroes like panthers from the dead King's hut. His weary old nurse has already been paid with death, as her nursing fee. Then the harem door shuts, and behind it are a dozen wives cooped up like animals for sacrifice.

" The ' red sunset ' begins. The nurse's blood has flowed, another victim dies as the royal corpse crosses the threshold, then the whole Via Dolorosa to the tomb is painted red. Another life is sacrificed as the corpse passes the town gate, then death follows death, till the tomb is reached. Down in the huge pit are deaths from suffocation, and up in the sunlight, on the new-made mound of earth, there is a thing called ' the blood plaster.' "

" A young Chinese wife labours in child-birth, and after suffering untold torture at the hands of ignorant, unclean and evil women, she dies in agony. Her physical sufferings are but small when compared with the mental torture of anticipating the punishment meted to women who die at the hour when they give life. A pool of blood in hell is her portion, and her reward for the sorrows of motherhood. That lake is controlled by demons, and there is no escape, save by payments to the priest who, this time, accepts no tinfoil money. ' Pay me well,' he says to the mother, ' and I will suspend the figure of a paper woman within the great temple bell. Each time I strike it, the little figure will move, and the tormented woman will move also, and so may, in time, elbow her way out of the pool, and reach the bank. But you must pay me well.' "

" A child playing about the hills of Tibet is called home to his tent one day, to find a group of maroon-clad lamas sitting there. Some important business is on hand, and the little fellow stands amazed to find himself the centre of interest and reverence.

" ' At last,' the lamas say, ' the spirit of the old Living Buddha who died five years ago in the Lama-sery of the Western Parks, has been traced.'

" For the whole of this period they consulted the oracles, discussed and conferred and now, at last, they have found the child who is the new incarnation. This is the boy who was born at the moment when the old man died, and in whom his spirit was re-incarnated. Then to the child's delight they open their bundles and bring out an offering of turquoises, peacock feathers and precious stones.

" Thus the child leaves his tent home and begins a new life. He now passes his days in a dark, malignant lamasery, and they are filled with the recital of liturgies, rosaries, prayers and incantations. Segregated from life's normal claims and interests, the years go by, and he becomes past master in the wiles of priest-craft, and the occult arts. This is the representation of god, and the symbol of satanic worship, to whom the crowds yield homage at the yearly festival—a ghastly travesty of God incarnate.

"A visitor* at the Red Lama Temple, near Peking, put into words the sensations she experienced when the ritual of that sinister worship was in progress :

" ' The chief lama, powerful, strongly built, and of great stature, towered above his assistants, who opened the service with a chant, in which the boys joined.

" ' There was a pause.

" ' And then the huge figure opened his mouth. I have never heard so cruel, so hypnotic, so vibrant a voice. It was as though all humanity and tenderness, all recollection of kindly things, had been wiped out. And yet it held a dominance that scorched and seared. My senses began to prickle, the air grew close, I was suddenly and desperately afraid. . . . Evil had been loosed—distinct—palpable. . . . For an awful moment I had a prevision of the damned.

" ' " I must get out," I said, and stumbled, somehow, to the door. . . . ' "

"Among the ranges of the Tibetan Alps are caves, some inhabited by wild beasts, and some by men—ascetics, who, dissatisfied with the mitigated gloom of lama life, have taken themselves to a lonelier existence in the caves of the earth. The deeper the gloom, the greater the merit of the anchorite, and when darkness has destroyed his eyesight, so that light becomes torture, he has attained his desired end.

*Mrs. Cecil Chesterton, " Young China and New Japan." Harrap.

Yet even the ascetic cave-dweller has not completely satisfied that Satan-inspired demand which would take from life the liberty and fullness which is the birthright of every human being. In the further depths of Inner Tibet, are monasteries, whose courtyard walls are pierced with stone-sealed apertures, behind which languish the immured monks of the Order. They sit in their tombs and turn a prayer-wheel. The endless night of their imprisonment is measured only by the knock given once each day, to tell that the bowl of water and morsel of bread, which just suffices to withhold the victim from the release of death, has been placed within reach. As time goes on, the stone is moved with increasing difficulty by the devitalised hand, and some day there will be no response, for death of the body will have consummated that of the soul."

When the younger man had read the paper through, he sat and pondered the mystery of godlessness. He saw the direct path of the ray of light, and the circuitous meanderings of ways that are dark.

He saw the blinding of the mind that could lead a merchant to try and release his mother's soul by tricking demons with gilt paper; the cruelty which condemns a child widow to a life of ignominy; the boastful glorying in murder and blood lust of revolting funeral rites; the distorted worship which exalts fecundity, but pours obloquy upon woman; the climax of horror where an entombed lama turns a prayer-wheel in his grave.

Knowing something of the masquerade which wears a sequin garment and calls itself an angel of

79

light, he feared that dazzle even more than these gross manifestations of evil, but as an Ambassador who dares not evade the direct warfare, he must study how to unmask all the subterfuges.

Turning to his friend, he said : " Tell me, where is the touchstone which unfailingly distinguishes the true from the false ?

" How can I learn to approach the captives with the message I have for them ?

" How can I avoid fear and keep free of panic in the face of such a foe ? "

His friend's reply was :

" The answer to the first, is—the touchstone is Christ and its application, ' What think ye of Him ? '

" As to the second, the story of the Good Shepherd teaches how to approach a sinner—he must be sought, rescued, tended and rejoiced over.

" As regards the third, you must put on the whole panoply of God, be strong in the Lord and in the power of His might, and know that nothing can by any means hurt you."

After that they prayed together, then parted in silence. At the door, the elder man slipped into the hand of the younger a volume, by a most unexpected author, with a marker at the following passage :

" The philosopher walked among a crowd in a market place, and overhead was a tight rope on which an acrobat was to perform an almost impossible feat of daring.

" The rope dancer commenced his performance. He had come out at a little door, and was going along a rope which was stretched between two towers, so that it hung above the market place and the people.

When he was just midway across, the little door
opened once more, and a gaudily-dressed fellow, like
a buffoon, sprang out, and went rapidly after the first
one.

" ' Go on, halt-foot,' cried his frightful voice.
' Go on, lazy-bones, interloper, sallow face ! Lest
I tickle thee with my heel. What dost thou here
between the towers ? In the tower is the place for
thee. Thou shouldst be locked up ; to one better
than thyself, thou blockest the way.'

" And with every word he came nearer and nearer
the first one. When, however, he was but a step
behind, there happened the frightful thing which
made every mouth mute and every eye fixed. He
uttered a yell like a devil, and jumped over the other
one who was in his way. The latter, however, when
he thus saw his rival triumph, lost at the same time
his head and his footing on the rope ; he threw away
his pole, and shot downwards faster than it, like an
eddy of arms and legs into the depth.

" The market place and the people were like the sea
when the storm cometh on : they all flew back, and in
disorder, especially where the body was about to fall."

In the margin was written the following note :

" The tormentor never touched his victim, nor
could he ever have touched him. He relied entirely
upon terrorising him, and fear was the only weapon
he handled.

" With his mind steadied by God, with his heart
garrisoned by His peace, and with his eye fixed where
it should be fixed, Christ's Ambassador is absolutely
safe, even though his commission take him where
Satan's seat is."

What is his Poise ?

ONE of the missionary societies includes in the questionnaire for referees who stand as guarantors of a candidate's good faith, this enquiry :

" What is the poise of his mind toward life ? " thus suggesting that they wish to know how the candidate's mental balance tips—toward caution or recklessness, selfishness or generosity, whether he is passionate or calculating, adaptable or rigid, a man of parts or a man of one idea, versatile or concentrated, exclusive or approachable.

There is no suggestion in the question, nor doubtless in the minds of those who drafted it, that any one of these characteristics make a man unsuitable for missionary work, but in meeting him, it is important that the Committee should know what his friends think of him, and they would quite rightly be suspicious of anyone whose record declared him to be perfectly balanced and accurately poised in every particular.

Give a man but a decade on the mission field, and there will be no further question as to the category in which he should be placed, for by that time the smallest bent on any specified line has become a strong characteristic, and will probably give him a

direction for life. The wise man is he who knows
his own bent, who mistrusts his temperament
and works toward the strengthening of his weak
point.

Missionaries are, generally speaking, a company of
strenuous people, and the intense look with which
they emit the word " Persia," " China," " Gobi,"
" Zanzibar," " the untouchable," " the leper," or
any other word which indicates their particular
line of interest, reveals an abnormal absorption into
one channel of service. The mesmeric force of that
glance controls the direction of every conversation in
which they take part.

Whether they be in a railway carriage, a drawing-
room or in their own mission station, they humbly
dominate their surroundings, and every topic is
diverted to the object of their own compelling interest.
It is this which makes of the missionary body a
peculiar people, and creates in the mission station
an atmosphere which can be compared with nothing
else on earth.

This absorption is not conducive to a normal, fully-
rounded life, developed evenly on all sides, and under
its influence the newcomer leans more and more
toward his own propensity or what the society
calls his " poise." If that poise be toward ease and
slackness, he finds good opportunity of indulging it,
for he is his own master, and there is no disciplinary
organisation to keep him up to the mark as there
was in the hospital or business house at home, and
certainly no Easterner will be annoyed with him for
being easy going. If, on the other hand, he has the
disposition of a disciplinarian and his bent is toward

severity, there will probably be nothing to divert him from becoming a ceaseless worker, and from developing a passion for organising other people's lives on the same plan of concentration.

If the young missionary is a good giver he is subject to a most subtle danger, for the Easterner has the parasitical *flair* for a good host, and seems to draw life from his vitality. Every relationship that he establishes, every adjustment that he makes, becomes a channel through which he pours himself out, in answer to the perpetual demands of people who make claims on him. Determined conscientiously to do his missionary work up to the hilt, he thinks that he must be accessible to all people and at all times.

For long hours he sits listening to interminable talk, and opens his fund of sympathy to every demand made on it. Though he has learnt by experience not to give money, he tries to make up by lavish giving of himself. In the course of ten years, he has reached the point where he has no personal rights left at all. His time and his strength are absolutely at the disposal of anyone who claims them, and besides being confidant and adviser to the Church, he is general benefactor to the whole town, and the whole town loves him for it. Where there is a family quarrel he acts as arbitrator, being the only man whom both parties entirely trust. If the quarrel has ended in blows, he is the doctor who binds up the wounds. From just arbitrator he becomes the loving counsellor who exhorts the disputers to live at peace one with another. He sees that the young student, who was the cause of the quarrel, is out of touch with his surroundings, and that his mind is full of immature and crude aspirations, so he further determines to make a friend of him, knowing that he alone, in the whole circle, can help him. Thus he is always extending the sphere of his contacts until he is overwhelmed by them.

Besides being preacher, teacher, superintendent of the outstations, first-aid man, director of the Boys' School, and amateur sanitary inspector, he has, on occasion, to turn his hand to building, to the digging of wells, to the buying and selling of his necessary teams of beasts, and, most exacting of all, be ready to receive all who come to him.

Thus, for years he becomes more and more deeply involved, until the mission station is the centre to which everyone in the locality turns in time of trouble.

In the process, he has gained a thorough knowledge of the people, he has learned to love them, somehow they are more his own people than his home people are, for he really has shared the intimacies of their joys and sorrows. Incidentally, he has so mastered their idiom, that he catches every shade of meaning in a story, and he is literally bearing the sorrows of hundreds of men and women. The spiritual darkness of this heathen land is a perpetual burden on his spirit, the failure of a Christian in an hour of testing, the callousness of a hardened sinner, the cruel misunderstanding of his intentions when, for conscience' sake, he refuses the help which it would be possible to give ; all these things oppress him and cause him many a sleepless night.

The time comes when his physical being can stand

the strain no longer, and the pull up comes with an inevitable visit to the doctor, who tells him plainly that he is badly run down, questions him about his way of life, and, incidentally, asks what he eats. The answer to this question is fairly satisfactory, because, although he eats natively prepared food, it is, if simple, quite wholesome, and the splendid air and sunlight make up for much that is lacking. The doctor presses the point further, and asks how he gets his meals. He now has to confess that he hardly knows what it is to eat uninterruptedly, for certain people know his meal times, and come then to be sure of finding him at home.

He admits that he is not sleeping well, and that he goes to bed late, because it is only when everyone else is in bed, that he can ever get an hour to pray. He has to be up early because there are few mornings when someone is not sitting at the courtyard door, waiting for it to open. He confesses that the whole thing has got a bit on his nerves, and that he can get no peace of mind until he has met every claim, and given each man what he wanted.

The doctor next asks him what hobby he has, and the missionary smiles a little grimly. He once had one, but it is years since he indulged it.

" Have you tried reading an interesting book before you go to bed, so as to break the tension ? " the doctor asks.

The man cannot remember when he last read a book for diversion. Every morning he leads family prayers, and his last piece of work before going to bed, is to read over the portion about which he must speak next day.

" How long is it since you had a good holiday ? " the doctor asks.

It is five years since he allowed himself leisure to go to the coast, and then he fitted it in with a Missionary Conference, so that the days were largely filled with meetings.

" Which day of the seven is your Sabbath ? " asks the doctor.

" Why, Sunday, of course," he replies, " I am not a Seventh Day Adventist."

" What do you do on that day ? "

The missionary tells him and, in the telling, he realises that Sunday is but the triple-distilled essence of the burdens of the week—more meetings, longer meetings, more interviews, longer interviews, till he dreads the day, and would rather, if he spoke the truth, face any other of the seven.

" Have you a friend with whom you can take a holiday, perhaps tramping about the hills ? "

The missionary reflects, and to himself he says : " I have fallen out of touch with ordinary life." Aloud, he answers : " I live alone, and that does not conduce to sociability. I did tramp out occasionally, but as soon as I appeared, a crowd gathered, and where there is a crowd there is opportunity, and where there is an opportunity for preaching I dare not neglect it."

" Well, young man, I see you will have to think things out for yourself. I cannot compel you to be a normal creature, but I *can* tell you that you are not fashioning yourself to the pattern of your Master. You go back and read the Gospels again, bearing it in mind that you are to readjust your life to that perfect pattern. Christ's life was not one hectic rush like yours. Why, *you* would never give yourself leisure to look at a lily of the field and draw a parable from it."

The doctor went home, and said to his wife : " Another fine man heading for breakdown. It is of no use to talk to him. He is one of those to whom advice is of very little use."

The missionary went back to his comfortless house : in the courtyard sat an old man who jumped up at his approach. " My son has taken opium," he said. " He is now unconscious. I beseech you to come at once and save him."

Off he went to a distant village, and worked for five hours to save that man's life. As soon as he could leave him, he did so. He had missed his lunch, and was too weary to enjoy the evening meal which was certainly not so appetising as usual. Before he finished it, his servant ushered in a group of young students, who sat with him for two hours. When they left it was time for evening prayers, and a village leader stayed behind to consult him about a very difficult case in his district.

At last he got to his room, and instinctively put out his hand for his Bible to read over to-morrow morning's subject for prayers. It seemed to him like a month since he saw that doctor ; he had so completely forgotten his own needs in sharing the difficulties of others.

A few days later, the doctor rode over after breakfast, and in passing, he spoke to the door-keeper.

" Obstruct all callers," he said, " until I leave. Your master has an important interview on hand, and must not be interrupted for anyone."

He walked straight to the living-room and sat down, waiting till the missionary had dispatched his first lot of business and could come to him. For the next three hours there was straight talk, and the younger man's mind and conscience were so busy that he had no leisure to wonder how it was that no callers came that day.

" I see you will take no heed of me as a doctor," his senior said at last ; " so now I speak to you as a prophet. Let me tell you that it is not because you are a Christian that you can break the law of God with impunity. What do you teach these converts of yours, is the commandment of God regarding the balance of labour and rest ? "

" Six days shalt thou labour," the missionary meekly answered.

" Then how do you reconcile it with your conscience to labour for seven days ? "

The missionary was silent, for he had no excuse to offer, but he began to think.

" I am not going to preach to you," the doctor continued, " but I am going to tell you a story, and I am not going to explain it, because you can think it out for yourself. You have a good mind, though you neglect it so shockingly.

" A certain lighthouse stood on arid ground, and the people who strove to make a living in this barren place, were always on the verge of starvation. The lighthouse keepers were good men and, touched to the quick by the sufferings of their neighbours, they gave away all that was anything more than a necessity of life to themselves. The people, realising their sympathy, would come again and again, begging a few drops of the oil, which was supplied to feed the lighthouse lamp, and the kind lighthouse keepers gave and gave until the day when, going to trim the lamp, they discovered that there was no oil left with which to fill it. Then the light, upon which the mariners relied to steer their course, failed them, and strange to relate, it was because of the unselfishness and the kindness of the lamp keepers."

The old doctor paused and looked at his young friend :

" You are the best example I have ever met of those lighthouse men. Your intentions are so good, your actions so humane, your devotion so pure, that not only you but everyone else is blinded to the danger you are becoming to the community. You, yourself, were set here as a beacon, and if the light that is in you be darkness, how great is that darkness ? "

The Right to Romance

"A DANGER to the people around you." He had never heard himself spoken of like that before. On the contrary, he always heard Europeans recognise, and natives applaud, his zeal, his earnestness, his intensity, his devotion and his spirituality. He had never for one moment fallen into the snare of seeking the praise of men, but he could not help knowing some of the things which they said about him.

One dart went home and that was the word about the observance of a day of rest. He really had no excuse to offer on that score and he forthwith determined conscientiously to set apart one day in seven for rest. His mind recoiled from the very word and he pictured himself spending a day of inaction, shut up in his room and refusing to see anyone, but with a restless, turbulent mind, realising only too well that he was giving offence to all who were turned away.

The first rest day was a complete fiasco. He felt like a prisoner behind shut doors and his attempts to read, write, or even meditate were perpetually interrupted by the voice of his boy at the courtyard door telling visitors : " The Reverend is sleeping."

If only he had a friend with whom he could tramp

they might find some interest in common, but somehow men looked on him as rather a crank and generally left him alone, for he had been so uncompromising, refusing to touch any side of normal social life, that now they all let him go his own way.

However the " day of rest " had become a matter of principle and the following week when it came round, he slipped out early, and spent most of the day on a lonely tramp among the hills. This outing, though not exactly enjoyable, supplied a change and was decidedly an improvement on sitting in his room.

The doctor, meanwhile, was doing a little wire-pulling, as a result of which a young engineer, several years junior to the missionary, paid him a visit.

" Can you find time to do me a favour ? " he began.

" Why, of course, what can I do for you ? "

" I have to go to the small encampment beyond the mountain pass. Would you help me to find an interpreter ? "

" Which day do you want to go ? "

" Any day next week would suit me."

" Well, if you can make it Monday, I'll go myself."

" Why, that's awfully good of you. Monday it shall be."

The result of that one day of relaxation was contact with this other man, who arranged to join him again on his next off day. The joy of companionship opened up a vista of pleasures ahead to which he looked forward with avidity. Before long that other fellow was taking three weeks' holiday in the hills and, unbelievably, they decided to go together.

The doctor chuckled with glee as he saw how well his prescription was working without even the need of a tonic, for his patient returned tanned, fit, sleeping well and facing life with renewed zest. He had even developed a hobby, for his friend lent him a camera and the two men rigged up a dark room where they spent hours experimenting with their films.

The one day of rest a week gradually became such a precious possession that he entered on the other six with a flying leap. His *entourage* adapted themselves amazingly to the fact that for one day in seven he was inaccessible and he began to enjoy his work as he had not enjoyed it for years. All his contacts were revivified by the freshness which he brought to them.

The following hot season he took another short holiday and this time he stayed with an old chum and his wife. The atmosphere of the house was delightful to him and the sight of his friend's radiant happiness and complete enjoyment of the two children, forced him to question one of his strongest principles, that of the principle of asceticism as an inevitable corollary of worthy missionary life. Here was an ideal Christian home with two small children growing up in it and its whole beautiful setting was a pattern to the native Church of what the relationship between man and wife should be, and an illustration of the responsibilities of Christian parenthood.

He heard the natives talk about it, saw how deeply interested they were and how they discussed this unusual thing together. The protective care which the man gave to his wife, his consistent courtesy, the obvious enjoyment by each of the other's company, the training of their children to instant obedience, the corrections without anger—it was obvious that all this made far more impression than many a sermon. He saw for himself how fine, how normal, how exemplary such a life was for a Christian missionary.

Was he after all mistaken in his devotion to austerity and asceticism ? Was he imposing on himself, to no purpose, a restraint which was really valueless ? Was he repressing instincts which, if he followed them, would lead him out into a larger life ?

Marriage, home, children, companionship, the joys of friendship and the gentle social pleasures of life—had he no right to these things ? Was there to be no room for romance in his life ?

He returned to his station and for many months pondered these questions. Indeed he had no opportunity of dismissing them from his mind because of the constant news of engagements formed between people who had met at that hill station. Obviously everyone seemed to think it quite right to meet, fall in love on slight acquaintance, become engaged and marry within a few months. It was the next step that he recoiled from—that settling down to the ease of a comfortable and ordinary life.

He thought with pain of two men who in College days had dedicated themselves to pioneer work and who at this hour were cosy, easy-chair parsons, having a far slacker time here than they could have had at home, where more would be expected of them. The call to adventurous life was stifled. The claims of the children, the man's creature comforts, the woman's love of house and home, the intense care for each other's well-being, had soon crowded out the sterner demands of missionary life. No, anything better than that.

He went on to think of the communities which exact a vow of celibacy from all who join them. He had an instinctive admiration for that point of view, yet, looking at it in the light of experience he felt there was something wrong there too. He shrank from the rigidity of placing oneself under a vow, for he scented danger in that direction. On the other hand he was prepared to admit that it was sometimes needful to bind the sacrifice with the cords of a personal vow, even to the horns of the altar. What of the men appointed by God to hazardous service, to live dangerously, perhaps to be pioneers in difficult places where, obviously, wife and child ought not to be taken ?

Moreover, the uncompromising words of the pioneer missionary Paul, had to be accounted for.

* "An unmarried man's business is about the Lord's business—how to please the Lord ; but a married man is anxious about the concerns of the world— how to please his wife, and he is drawn two ways. And the unmarried woman is anxious about the Lord's business—to be holy both in body and spirit ; but the married woman is anxious about the concerns of the world—how to please her husband.

"'This I say in your own interest; not to put shackles on you, but to promote seemliness and undistracted devotion to the Lord."

He pondered the whole difficult question, seeing on one hand the man who was spoilt by marriage and on the other, the man who was made by it. He saw

* 1 Cor. vii. 33, 34, Weymouth translation.

the value of the home and he saw the danger of the home. Though he could not but deprecate the haste, the precipitancy with which newcomers established understandings so that from the first they never had a free heart and mind for the people to whom they came, yet he admitted his own mistakes and knew that he too had erred. Nevertheless he was glad that his poise inclined toward the side of austerity.

It seemed to him so unworthy, when a young fellow confided to him that he was proposing hastily to a girl, lest someone else get her. Had the man no place for God's control in his life ? Had he so little knowledge of himself and human nature as to think that a passing inclination represented guidance for one of the most important steps of life ? It was quite patent to outsiders which of the many marriages were made in heaven and bore the hall-mark of Divine approval, and which were of the rolled gold variety whose thin veneer of deceptive value soon wore off at the edges, exposing patches of the baser metal to view. The price of momentary physical attraction was often paid in the coin of life-long fundamental antagonism.

Months of thought, prayer, fasting and meditation brought him to a decision and he made the following note in his diary : " Marriage is the Divine intention for man and woman. Obviously the sphere is more complete in form than a hemisphere could possibly be. Only God can direct a man to his true partner and God only can join them perfectly. Christian home life is an invaluable witness to the natives of a Christless land. Another demand, however, is made on those whose vocation is that of pioneer—pathfinder and roadmaker—on those who go ahead to make it possible for others to follow. Men and women of the vanguard may need to deny themselves even the necessities of life, to say nothing of its softer though perfectly legitimate pleasures.

" The duty of such is literally to endure hardness, to be good soldiers unencumbered by the things of this life, athletes unentangled by any weight. It may well be that such exacting demands are only made on the few (the New Testament is the text-book on that subject) but there are certainly some on whom they are made and I . . . It is a vocation, a calling, an ordination to special service.

" Every man and woman has the right to romance but some must be prepared to forego that right for the sake of Christ and His gospel."

" I tell you in truth," said Jesus, " that there is no one who has left house or wife, or brothers or parents or children, for the sake of God's Kingdom, who shall not receive many times as much in this life, and in the age that is coming, eternal life."

The Department comes under Criticism

Mr. G. K. Chesterton, in a pithy essay, demonstrates the supreme value of the British jury system by virtue of which, when a really serious decision has to be made, and a man may even be on trial for his life, the verdict is taken out of the hands of experts, and men accustomed to the procedure of law courts, and committed to twelve ordinary people summoned from the daily avocations of life.

They are asked to sit down while all the details of the case are stated in their presence and are then sent off by themselves to decide what they think about it. The whole proceeding is sane and sensible because the twelve men have no professional reputation to guard, no personal axe to grind, and there is nothing to divert them from viewing the case with the simple directness of the man on the street.

Because of that same unprofessional detachment of outlook, groups of Christian laymen, directing their attention to the problems of the mission field, can offer sound advice even to Boards of specialists on the matter of fundamental policies and the methods by which they should be put into action.

The Christian onlooker can often see mistakes with a clearness which has become impossible to those

who are engrossed in the task. To be of supreme
value, however, the members of the Commission
must, like the members of the jury, be free from any
preconceived ideas, and should also conduct their
enquiries not from London Board rooms nor even
from the westernised surroundings of a coastal town
or hill station, but in direct contact with the missionaries themselves in inland conditions.

Laymen's Commissions have visited each of the
mission fields from time to time, but the most search-
ing enquiry, resulting in the most revolutionary
suggestions, proceeded from a plain business man
who made an unheralded journey to the East, stepped
in and out of a number of mission stations, spent days
in talk with experienced missionaries, tramped their
districts with them, then brought the whole concentration of his simple, shrewd, powerful mind to
bear upon the problems of the case. Himself a
whole-hearted Christian and a successful merchant,
the advance of Christ's Kingdom was the passion of
his life.

Moreover, having made a considerable fortune he
felt the responsibility of stewardship and was there
in order to see for himself how and where he was
justified in using his money in the furtherance of
world evangelism.

His was the type of mind which can absorb an
immense amount of detailed information and reduce
it to main principles. He at once detected weakness :

" The work is good as far as it goes," he wrote,
" but its weakness lies in the fact that it is too indi-
vidualistic. . . . It is strong or weak, just as branch
businesses are strong or weak as they are left to the

charge of men of varying capacity with no definite policy to guide them and with none of the . . . helps which a big business concern, or a great missionary society, should give. . . . These would tend to link weakness to strength and substitute continuity for wastage. . . . New conditions are calling for new plans. . . . Some societies are all right for pioneer work but do not know how to occupy territory effectively, others are engrossed in institutional work and have little opportunity for direct evangelism."

He firmly protested against the widely accepted policy of establishing a Church as an exotic institution on a denominational basis, which policy led to waste of money, of time and of life, producing a native Church which could never be left to carry on without its foreign founder.

The while the experts spoke to him of need for reinforcements of men and more money to support them, this practical investigator was asking :

" For how many years has this station been open?"

He generally received the answer :

" It has been opened twenty, thirty or forty years."

" What prospect is there of withdrawing the missionary from this centre to give another locality a chance ? "

In every case he was assured that it was too early for such a move to be considered

" The native," they said, " makes an excellent ' helper,' but when left in charge of the concern, or in control of the finances, is not to be relied on."

Then he saw that while *he* was concerned with the Church as the body of believers, *they* were talking about a foreign organisation, commonly spoken of as " the Church " but including a large compound, a Church building, schools and divers institutions all of which were in perpetual need of support from foreign funds.

Now he saw that, if he gave the large donations which their method of administration required, he was but putting silver and gold into a bottomless pit— the upkeep of a Westernised mission compound in an Eastern town. This might be maintained *ad infinitum* but would never bring about the evangelisation of the world in this, or in any other generation.

He went home, put pen to paper and wrote an epoch-making Survey in which he indicted the Mission Boards for what he called their special weakness— absence of a plan which would make possible the evangelisation of the world.

" Missionaries," he stated, " are casual labourers if not building on a plan which is recognised by their societies. . . . If I were asked to state in a word the special weakness of missionary work I should say it has no plan, and in my judgment nothing else compares with this in importance. . . . Without recognised plan each man is liable to destroy the work of his predecessor. . . . If anyone has had experience in building a house he knows that it is the ground plan which counts."

Simultaneously an Anglican clergyman produced a startling book which reviewed the scriptural method of missionary work in the first century, and called on the societies to revise their policies by comparing them with the methods used by St. Paul who so conspicuously trusted the Holy Spirit for the upbuilding of the Church.

The result of this helpful criticism was a new viewpoint and a fount of new thought which demanded new words for its expression. Very soon missionaries began to talk of " Indigenous Church methods " in contradistinction to those generally accepted, whereby the missionary remained permanently in charge of the Church which had been established, and would never consider leaving it unless his successor appeared on the scene.

The Boards foresaw difficulties and the discussion of " Paul's methods or Ours " was not encouraged in conference. But the whole body of missionaries began to think along these lines. Some vigorously approved the suggestions, others violently opposed them ; a few determined to try them, but the majority said : " It is a splendid ideal, but in *my* station it most certainly would not work."

Nevertheless a seed had been sown and, as is the way with seeds, it germinated, and its growth has been prodigious. To-day the words Indigenous Church, Paul's methods, World Dominion policies, are heard on all sides, and have come to stand for an attitude toward world evangelism.

The whole language and vocabulary connected with foreign missionary work is eloquent of mistaken relationships. It is expressive of the planting of a denomination in a foreign field, but not of the establishment of Christ's Church among a people who were made for Himself but never knew it.

" Our field," " Our station," " Our Christians," " My Evangelist," " My Bible woman," " We are urging the Church to become indigenous," " I am always hoping that the Church will become strong enough for me to be able to hand over," "We have adopted a policy of devolution."

The whole phraseology reveals the egocentric outlook, for were the view Christocentric the language would inevitably change and the possessive pronoun would become conspicuous by its absence.

What is the right thought and conception of the missionary's work in an unevangelised country ?

1. He is an Ambassador bearing a message from his King.

2. He is a preacher, but not a preacher of sermons —a preacher of the Gospel.

3. He is a sower. A sower of thoughts whose harvest is actions.

4. He is a teacher, and as such must not only tell people how to be saved but undertake the exacting task of declaring to them the whole counsel of God. " The missionary preaches, but it is Christ who saves the soul. The missionary teaches, but it is Christ who builds His Church. . . . Our answer to the question ' What must I do to be saved ? ' has been clear and unequivocal and we have never doubted Christ's power to save the most sinful and the most ignorant, but to the question ' What must we saved ones do, to become a Church ? ' we have shrunk from giving as definite an answer."

Only soundness of thought can lead to soundness of method and the best way to gain soundness of thought is to turn back to the Scriptures and try to see how St. Paul understood his commission and by what means he set about to put it into execution.

His was a simple plan and one which relied entirely

on the work of the Holy Spirit in the individual and in the Church. Since the command was that the Gospel of Jesus Christ was to be preached to every creature it must follow that some means would be supplied whereby the command might be carried into execution, a thing which could never be if it must depend on the efforts of " foreign missionaries." The native converts built up by the Holy Spirit into a living organism called the Church, are appointed to evangelise and teach as they themselves have been evangelised and taught, and should, in turn, become missionaries to other tribes.

As regards the upbuilding of each Church, it is the work of the Holy Spirit, by Whose grace every member is endowed with such spiritual gifts as are necessary to that upbuilding. The Holy Spirit Himself is the Teacher of the converts—He is able to sustain them, to guide them into all truth and give them their inheritance among the saints. They may therefore safely be left to His care and to the keeping power of Christ, when once the missionary Ambassador has proclaimed to them the word of reconciliation and declared to them the whole counsel of God.

St. Paul acted thus at Ephesus, even though he was obliged to say : " I know that when I am gone, fierce wolves will get in among you, and they will not spare the flock ; yes, and men of your own number will arise with perversions of the truth to draw the disciples after them. So be on the alert . . . I entrust you to God and the word of His grace ; He is able to upbuild you. . . ."

There is a most profound difference between the

missionary who is so convinced that Christ's salvation is unto all men that he cannot for a moment admit to his mind any thought but that the Holy Spirit will instruct, guide, illumine and confirm all who place their trust in Christ, bringing the whole body of the Church to maturity and perfection, whether its individual members be Eastern or Western, Negroid or Nordic, and on the other hand the man who believes that not only the planting but the growth and the fruition depend upon his care and oversight.

Books to be Read on this subject

A Study of Foreign Missions. From a layman to laymen and others.

The Indigenous Church.

Indigenous Fruits.

By Sidney J. W. Clark. Price 6*d.* each.

Missionary Methods—St. Paul's or Ours.

The Spontaneous Expansion of the Church.

By Roland Allen. Price 3*s.* 6*d.* each.

World Dominion. A Quarterly International Review of Christian Progress. Price 1*s.* Publishers: World Dominion Press, Mildmay, London, N.1.

So does the Junior

WHILE the members of the Mission Boards are sitting round long tables in oak-panelled rooms, considering the piles of papers which concern the candidates whose applications are under consideration, those same candidates are holding a coffee party in a student's room, to discuss the Boards to which they have applied.

The microphone and the loud speaker have their uses and their abuses, but no use could be more valuable than a connection between those two assemblies, enabling each to hear the comments of the other. It is certain that by no other means will either group have the benefit of seeing the other as the other sees him.

The students think they know a lot, they have bombarded every available missionary with questions and have unerringly detected which of them were candid in their answers and which were out to bluff.

When they make an offer they sometimes approach the Board straightforwardly with the question : "If I join this Society shall I be appointed to the staff of an existing station, or may I be released for direct evangelism ? "

Some are even prepared to withdraw their offer of

service if the answer they receive appears ambiguous. Yet were the Mission Boards in turn to ask their young catechisers what they understand by the terms "Direct Evangelism," "Indigenous Church Methods" and "World Dominion Principles" the answer would be exceedingly vague, for these words represent things which no man understands until he puts his own hand to the task of working them out.

There is even sometimes a strange confusion in the mind of the candidate between the words "Indigenous Church Methods" and "Pioneer Evangelism." Yet the two must never be confused.

The study of a good dictionary would be of great value to the young recruit. He would read there :

"Pioneer—a man with a pickaxe or a spade whose business is to march before an army, to make or repair roads, clear them of obstructions and work at entrenchments or bridge-building."

Thus few men only are called to be pioneers though every missionary is concerned with the planting of an indigenous church. The pioneer must always think of those who follow and not of his own achievement. His work is the levelling of roads and the building of bridges. The establishment of intercourse and making first contacts with primitive people is the levelling of roads, and the construction of grammars and dictionaries can be compared with the building of bridges, for they span the unnavigable river which flows between men who have no language in common.

These are the lines of communication on which the army is going forward to the accomplishment of the task which the pioneer saw and prepared for, but probably never completed himself.

The fact is that God does not tell a youngster at home that He is going to make him a pioneer missionary. What He does is to appoint him as His Ambassador in a foreign land. The real training has scarcely begun, and it is a safe rule that the first five years should be spent as learner, observer, subordinate and listener, the active contribution of that period being to give ungrudging help anywhere, anyhow, and to anyone as required. The pioneer calling is a re-commission and comes to one whom God has set apart to that work.

Indeed, a missionary society does a young man serious wrong if it allows him to undertake pioneering before he has language and experience sufficient for the job, for his mistakes may handicap his whole future influence, and the more enthusiastic he is, the more likely he will be to make them.

The personality of a great pioneer missionary and the unusual interest of the field he represents, always result in offers of service. The younger people whom he touches are fired with a desire for pioneer work.

When Sundar Singh came into contact with students, a new spirit of sacrifice was enkindled among them, and when he told them of the hardships he encountered in Tibet, the poverty of the food, the dirt and ignorance of the people and the dangers from robbers and in crossing glaciers and rivers, their reaction was to plan expeditions to accompany him on his journeys. On some occasions a few of them even started with him, but the difficulties of the way were too great and they returned.

These young enthusiasts were not sufficiently inured to hardship to stand the strain, and the effect of their abortive effort would be a serious handicap on future work. They had gone forward without Divine commission—a disastrous proceeding. In undertaking any future enterprise they would be made hesitant by a sense of shame at having turned back on this occasion, though it was probably the wisest thing to do. Moreover, the presence of these inexperienced companions, instead of being a help was an added danger and burden to the Sadhu himself.

Senior missionaries are not without experience of the intractability of youth, and, on the other hand, juniors are deeply conscious of the conservatism of middle-age. The result is friction.

It is just here that a deliberate process of mental adjustment is required, both in senior and junior, that each may come to see the other's point of view. The critical spirit which recognises no good in the work of the past, the conceit which sweeps away all time-honoured methods, the ingratitude which uses steps cut by others in the rocks of ignorance and superstition for personal advantage, is too often characteristic of the newcomer.

This has not passed unobserved and a cultured young Eastern woman, writing for recruits says: "Formerly the word 'Missionary' implied piety, kindness and goodness. To-day the same word provokes a different reaction and the question we now ask of each other is 'What kind of a Christian is this new worker, true or false?' The answer given is 'Wait and see.'" It is hard to build and easy to destroy, but the work of the demolisher is more dangerous than that of the builder.

While it is taken for granted by the senior that

the newcomer will be appointed to a post in some existing branch of the work, where, at the moment, he is greatly needed, the junior may have come with the determination to lose no time in sowing the seed of an indigenous church in an untilled field. Therefore his senior's proposal is met with unexpected opposition and occasionally with uncompromising refusal :

" I have determined never to touch institutional work," he says, " I believe in Paul's methods and I feel that God has called me to pioneer evangelism. That being so, I must not get entangled with station obligations and I wish to waste no time in getting to my job."

His senior is loath to behave in an arbitrary fashion, so he answers sympathetically and they sit down to talk it out together. The tired, overworked man is already involved in more station work than he can possibly cope with, and he had counted on every kind of assistance that a newcomer is able to contribute. This young man could be asked to teach English in the school, superintend the boys' games, help with station accounts and assist with correspondence. All these things which have seemed the last straw to the elder man would be so easily handled by the newcomer to whom they would afford a basis of intercourse with the natives and be even a relief from the long hours of language study.

If the young man gets his own way he generally goes off to a village and there tries his hand at direct evangelism. He inevitably flounders through inexperience, and if he be too opinionated to seek advice and too conceited to recognise his own wilfulness he probably makes but little headway.

It is an actual fact that some who have begun this way are, years later, still in the same little village where they started, and still out of touch with the people whom they have never understood. Far from becoming pioneers and clearing roads for the advance of an army, they have only succeeded in making the way more difficult for others.

By reason of ignorance and inexperience, they have failed in their contribution to the upbuilding of an indigenous church and some have returned home speaking of the area as a very discouraging field.

On the other hand, if he yields to his senior's advice and joins a station staff, the junior runs the risk of being absorbed into the routine of detail work. There are many instances of men who dreamed great dreams of taking part in the advancement of Christ's Kingdom, but who have spent their youth and strength in the toil of everyday duties, until they cannot lift themselves out of the rut of station work and, at the same time, have become slaves to its small comforts.

Between these two extremes there is a right way, and one which ensures the necessary discipline, training, equipment and mental adjustment essential to vital missionary work. If a man is ever to be of use in direct, constructive evangelism, he must somehow secure the necessary equipment for the task.

This equipment includes a good fund of fluent, easy, idiomatic language and familiarity with the ways and customs of the people. This requires such constant intercourse with them that he begins to think yellow, brown, black or red, according to the tint of his parishioners' skins. In a word, he must come to the point of feeling " at home " with them. On the physical plane he must acclimatise, and simultaneously become so accustomed to native food that he can, if required, live on it entirely. He must inure himself to the fatigues of travel, and he must learn how to conduct his life and business in an oriental way.

Determination to live a native life and eat nothing but native food, from the first day, has often led to a physical breakdown, in consequence of which the newcomer has merely added the burden of nursing him, to the duties of the already overworked staff.

Many would say that the first five years were the most difficult period of their whole missionary life. Awkwardness in language induces strain in social intercourse. Some beginners are diffident and only with tremendous effort force themselves to use even what they know of the tongue ; nervousness adding greatly to their difficulty in understanding it.

Food, and how to eat it, is an embarrassment. It entails the use of chopsticks, or fingers, instead of knife and fork, and this under the merciless scrutiny of observant natives.

The long weary hours which the newcomer spends listening to conversations of which he only understands an occasional word reach the limit of boredom, and it is not unlikely that he is kept at high nervous tension by having to sit in a most uncomfortable position, cross-legged or with knees flexed at a painful angle.

Sunday services, when only followed with difficulty, are a weariness to the flesh. Sermons are often dull and nearly always too long.

To slow down from an active life to this creeping

pace is a process of mental pain and to find oneself incapable of handling unaided the simplest matter, is a humbling business and naturally opens the door to the tormenting question : " Of what use am I here ? Would I not have rendered better service by staying at home ? "

Let no one be discouraged by these realistic details. All this is but an episode in the missionary life—a period which must be endured. Even if the first year be spent at a modern language school where life is far from dull, the period of adjustment is merely postponed, for if the man is ever going to be a missionary *indeed*, an Ambassador for Christ capable of delivering His message of reconciliation in terms that can be understood, and in a manner worthy of the King Who commissioned him, whether it be as doctor on a hospital staff, master in a school, or village evangelist, he must endure this process of adaptation to the view-point of the primitive mind.

All said and done, the disciplines spoken of are comparatively superficial, and deeper down there is a basic, fibre-toughening discipline which becomes part of a man's very being, and which is the result of a secret, personal austerity which chooses the hard way when the choice is known only to God and to the man who makes it.

" This sacred work demands, not lukewarm, selfish, slack souls, but hearts more finely tempered than steel, wills purer and harder than the diamond," wrote Père Didon.

" Endurance is a mental quality," said Captain Scott, and on that basis he selected the members of his Antarctic expedition.

" Training of the right kind of missionary begins in the nursery," says Amy Carmichael.

It is a life-long severity but it produces a man who can be relied on not to be brittle under strain, not to sag under discouragement and not to go slack when there is no one to supervise him. This is a strength which is not captured suddenly, " it is the offspring of the patient years," and in order to secure it, let no candidate for the mission field allow himself to view any imposed restrictions as irksome. They will come much harder on some than on others, and their superficial value may be greater or less, but their basic importance is beyond measure, for it is that of *discipline*.

" It is easy for the older folk to yarn about ' discipline,' but nowadays we are well trained in our professions, and do we need it ? "

" The university course, the hospital, the pedagogic training have placed us on a different footing to the old pioneers. Surely we can be let off things that were necessary to them. Moreover while it may still be useful to one who is expecting to be a pioneer, it is superfluous to the man who expects to live in conditions not unlike those of the West."

These are the comments made again and again at student squashes.

Quite true, if the making of himself an agent of a missionary society were all that a man expects in going abroad. But, if he be an Ambassador appointed by Christ Himself and vested with authority to represent Him in an enemy country ; if he be entrusted with terms of reconciliation to the captives, and at the same time be called to warfare against principalities and powers and against the rulers of the darkness of this world, then let him not despise any opportunity of using discipline as a means to an end.

" The evangelisation of the world is a desperate struggle with the prince of darkness and with everything his rage can stir up in the shape of obstacles, vexations, oppositions and hatred, whether by circumstances or by the hand of man."

Therefore seek wisdom and welcome discipline.

For Women Only

JOAN, Betty and Ann had all travelled together on a liner, eastward bound. They were all going out for the first time but not as members of the same Missionary Society, nor, indeed, were they even all going to the same country. For the next ten years they corresponded and, at the end of that time, all happened to be on furlough, so they celebrated the event by spending a week-end together at their old Training College.

At the Principal's invitation they met together in her study after dinner, to talk out their missionary experiences. When they had drawn their chairs round the fire there was silence as each one began to think of all that had happened since last they were together, and the inmost thought of each one was : " How different it has all been from what I expected."

The Principal was the first to speak : " I want to hear everything," she said, " but remember that what you have to tell can only be of value if shared on a basis of complete honesty."

To this they agreed, and Betty led off :

" The impress of the mission field on my life was taken during the first five years. The Society to which I belong puts young workers into a station where they are subject to the authority of a senior woman who is responsible for them. When she is of the right sort, this plan is a great success, but if she be a woman lacking in knowledge of how to handle a junior, it is just the reverse. The one to whom I was sent upset me straight off by constantly referring to me as ' my junior worker.' Notice the three words, ' my ' equals possession, ' junior ' equals inferiority, ' worker ' equals status. They were indicative of my place in her landscape.

" I don't deny that she was a fine, devoted woman, but I soon found out that, though she worshipped the one true God and was always exhorting others to do the same, there was a secret shrine in which she set up a small idol, and that idol was ' the work.'

" I often felt like the victim which was to be offered to that god. Anything I wanted specially to do, would, I was told, ' hurt the work.' We were all driving busy the whole time, in order to keep pace with ' the work.' Everyone was utterly absorbed in ' the work.'

" This hard-working senior took it for granted that she was entitled to exercise control over my personal liberty, and before long I realised that I was in danger of losing all initiative and becoming a mere robot. It seemed strange to me who had been responsible for myself, my words and my actions, to be under the control of a woman who not only expected to chaperon my body but my mind and my soul.

" I was scared, and thought I had made a complete hash of my life. Then, fearing lest I should go under, I rose up and resisted her. It was the hardest thing

I had yet lived through, and I used to call on God for deliverance. Though I had heard of ' peculiar difficulties ' on the mission field, no one had prepared me for this, which I now realise is no uncommon situation.

" There seemed to be no point of contact between us, though honestly I tried every way to find one. I would talk about College days or about our hiking tours just to make a diversion, but she never once rose to it. Then I wrote home for books, because the station bookshelf held nothing but biographies of long dead missionaries, but not once did she so far meet me as to borrow one of my books. In fact, I knew that she viewed reading as time stolen from ' the work.' I also knew that she mistrusted happiness, as not being good discipline.

" Strangely enough, though we had both signed the same basis of belief, our points of view were totally different and we had no fellowship in the things of the spirit. Even at family prayers I felt the devotional went under to ' the work.'

" I am sure that I was as big a trial to her as she was to me, and moreover I was sensitive about having been forced into what, after all, was her home, by people who never took the time or trouble to realise the obvious incompatibility of our temperaments. Those five years were a wretched time, during which I fought steadily against a domination to which, though I bowed my head, I never dared to yield in spirit.

" She spoke the language well and never rested until I did the same. Certainly all the slackness, self-pleasing and indulgence which may have been natural to me, were knocked out of me then, for if I resisted her in the inner man, it was the more incumbent on me to measure up to her high standard of conscientiousness and ' work.'

" After five years, as you know, I was moved, and then things were different, but that first experience has stamped me for life."

There was silence in the group as each woman present made her offering of unspoken sympathy to the once vivacious Betty, now so sobered and self-contained.

Joan came next in order, and this was her story :

" Nothing could be more different from Betty's, than my early experience. I started off with a real good time at the Language School. There were games, picnics, debates, squashes, and our study course was made as easy and delightful as it could be. It was like College, only the new surroundings made everything even more enjoyable.

" I had taken Arts, so I was put to school work straight off. The Head was a brick—competent, clever and advanced. She was only too glad that I should put my modern ideas into practice, and I thoroughly enjoyed doing so. We formed a missionary community of twelve households besides half a dozen Government Officials and business men with their families. All our houses were close together, and we saw a great deal of each other—too much.

" Everyone gave a party to welcome me to the community and we returned the hospitality. Then each family invited me to spend an evening that they might get to know me better. My music was an asset at their socials, and my tennis at their tennis parties. In this way, twelve whole months slipped by ; then came a long summer at a hill station, and by the end of the second winter, the restrictions of this life had so closed in on me that I gave personal offence if I tried to refuse an invitation.

" Then I realised that I had unconsciously formed the habit of giving my regular lessons in the school while I spent the rest of my time in trivial social intercourse. I gradually awoke to the fact that I was no missionary at all, nor likely to be, and I knew nothing more of my pupils than that they sat in rows before me at stated hours and for a stated purpose. The spiritual was rapidly dropping out, and I was less of a missionary than when I was at home. I tried to pull myself together, but found that something had dried up in me, and when I attempted to speak of spiritual things I had nothing to say. I even began to wonder what I had come out for. Life had lost all savour and I had lost my ideals. Yet the school girls were evidently not expecting more than I gave them, and most members of the community took this kind of life for granted.

" I was miserable, but I had not the spiritual courage to face it out. No one had ever warned me how easily and how quickly a young missionary may be diverted from her purpose. I did not feel that I could approach my competent Chief with a spiritual difficulty ; I was afraid she would not understand. Inwardly miserable as I was, the whole community began to get on my nerves. I realised that we were all far too much interested in each other's doings. Within three years the bondage had become intolerable, and I knew what an old missionary meant when she came to the Training College and said to us : 'Flee gossip like you flee the devil.' At the time I thought she was using strong language. Now I saw for myself that tittle-tattle was the curse of small circles.

"I was so involved in the net that I even had to distribute my calls in exact rotation lest I give offence to someone. Would you believe it, I actually brought myself to grovel to some touchy woman when she accused me of slighting her? I can tell you, Betty, that my fun did my soul more injury than your senior's domination ever did to yours.

"When things were at their very worst and I was considering sending in my resignation and going home, a woman passed through our station and stayed in our house. She was the kind of missionary I used to dream of—a real live wire, and contact with her gave me a high voltage shock. She saw in a moment what was wrong, and tackled me. I was in such desperate need and she was so kind and so concerned, that I told her everything. By way of my despair, my spiritual dryness and my hopeless confession of it all, she led me back to the Saviour and He restored my soul and renewed my first love.

"At that time I came into a new experience of the power of Christ to transform sterility into fruitfulness, drought into a spring of living water, and to give grace sufficient for the requirements of everyday life. Everything was changed. Formerly I had no message for the girls, but now the love of Christ constrained me, I could not help speaking, and things began to move."

"Tell us, Joan, how did all this affect the gossiping community?"

" It affected them vitally. That high-voltage woman spoke very straightly to some of them and I, of course, had to take a stand. This resulted in a parting of the ways, and some admitted that their missionary life had been a failure and that they had never had a message. Talking it over led to the formation of a Bible study circle, which was a tremendous help to all of us. As we prayed, things developed, and before long our dry station began to blossom as a rose."

It was Ann's turn next.

" That was great, Joan," she said. " We all knew that something tremendous had happened to you. To speak for myself, I must say that I am in love with my work and longing to get back to it, but I also have had my difficulties, only mine were not with my seniors, for they were saints, but with juniors, for I had two lively youngsters put to live with me five years ago."

" Good, now let us have the other side of the story," said Joan. " Report on your juniors, Ann, only be sure to give us the whole truth."

" Well, I had been so recently a junior myself that I thought I should understand their problems and that we might get on happily together. So we did on the whole, but I must say they were a rebellious and stiff-necked couple.

" I knew they must face spiritual issues, so from the first we prayed and talked together, and I felt they might be lonely, so I made time for recreation. Between us we collected an excellent library and we each contributed some natural gift to communal life. One was a musician and the other was a good reader, and what between singing, photography and the discussion and sharing of interests, both spiritual and temporal, we really came into the relation of a happy family."

" It sounds lovely," said Betty, " but where did the trouble come in ? "

" The first clash was over the matter of dress. Those two came forewarned against becoming missionary frumps, so they each brought an outfit of charming dresses and, along with the smart frocks, the make-up to which they were accustomed. I do not mean anything very serious, but just the touch of powder-puff and lipstick which they felt was needed to make them look nice.

" Now we lived in a place where white people were few, and our nearest Western neighbours were missionaries belonging to an Order which wears a habit. When my girls appeared in sleeveless frocks, low necks and short skirts, their general lack of covering shocked the natives. I heard of it and I spoke, begging them not to spoil their influence for the sake of a little adaptation in dress. They both instantly went off the deep end and told me that my control of them was to be limited to mission matters. Their dress and style had nothing whatever to do with me.

" I rather think they enjoyed the excitement, for they let out that someone had said : ' These frocks will make the old missionaries sit up,' so they were expecting it. They got their own way and I was worsted, for it was two against one, and I was no match for them.

" A little later, however, a native woman who was

coming to help us, made an excuse to stay away. I saw there was something behind it, and when the matter was investigated, I was told, and in very plain language, that her husband objected to let her work in a house where the women did not dress decently. In fact, there was an expression used which suggested that women who left their bodies so uncovered might go all lengths.

" The two of them were in the inner room, and they overheard and understood the whole conversation. They were furiously angry and rounded on *me*, saying that I ought to have explained matters to them more clearly than I did. From that day they certainly modified their style of dress, but the damage was done. I was thankful when, in a few months, they were moved to another station. I can tell you they departed sadder and wiser girls.

" I do not want you to think that they were extreme in their dress ; they just wore what many girls do wear in hot weather at the seaside, over here, but to the sari-swathed Indian woman they looked fast, and as for Moslem men—once you understand the things they say, it makes you super-careful.

" They were so afraid of being peculiar, yet they could not see that they looked both queer and eccentric to all the people who met them every day, did not admire them in the least, and utterly misjudged them.

" The strange thing was that when we read books on sacrifice together, they were most responsive and seemed ready for anything. Perhaps they were, provided they might choose their own line of sacrifice."

" I know what you mean," said Joan, " and the

same principle works in the matter of engagements. We, here, all know that the people of the East cannot understand freedom between the sexes. We had a typical case at our station. You remember Kathleen ? One summer she went to the hills and came back engaged to Harold. They promised her hostess that if they might meet in her house, they would be most discreet. One day they found they were being watched from a window by a group of students. They had merely been kissing each other as affectionately as an engaged couple would do at home, where no one would think anything of it. Harold was savage, but Kathleen rather laughed at the whole business.

" A few months later one of those very students was dismissed for bad behaviour with one of the nurses, and the excuse he gave was : ' When we saw your engaged couples kiss each other, we wanted to be very Western and we did the same. For us it was disastrous. It *may* be safe for you, but it is not so for us.'

" Kathleen and Harold were tremendously keen and seemed ready for any hardship, but, I suppose, as Ann says, they must choose their own form of sacrifice."

When each had had her say, the Principal spoke :

" You have added but little to the mass of diverse problems which are talked out in this room from time to time," she said. " Problems of human adjustments, problems of love and friendship, problems of racial intercourse, problems of spiritual declension.

" The solution of them all is on the spiritual plane,

but when a group of people of different up-bringing, outlook and social code are forced to live in abnormal proximity, they cannot with impunity break God's laws of psychology and mentality.

" Life, warped in any direction, tends to overstrain, overstrain leads to frayed nerves, and frayed nerves produce friction which is the end of harmony. Each of you found that your peculiar difficulty on the mission field was something quite unexpected, yet I tried to warn you and I begged every missionary who came here to do the same."

" We were warned," said Betty, " but the warnings were too vague and the real struggle found us unprepared."

" What form did you expect the opposition to take ? " asked the Principal. " Did you visualise a spectacular encounter ? Have you not yet learnt that the Satanic assault always comes from an unexpected quarter, and is so subtle that, like poison gas, it has stifled faith, paralysed effort and enveloped the victim in a thick cloud which blots out heaven and earth, before he has become sufficiently aware to be on the defensive ?

" Tactics learnt in the class-room are the sport of the enemy. It is on active warfare that the recruit learns how to parry the sly thrust, how to handle his gas mask and the exact use of each weapon of his warfare."

" Art Thou a God that doeth Wonders ? "

CHRIST'S Ambassador carries a declaration by which his Lord has pledged Himself to confirm by signs the word which His servant preaches. Is it to be relied on ?

Will there be evidences when he enters the great Indian *bazar*, the forbidding Chinese city, the South African mart, the oasis of the desert ? Will he see marvels as he travels by caravan, by river steamer, or treads the zig-zag jungle trail ?

What kind of thing will happen ? Will the dead live ? Will demons be cast out ? Will men be changed ? Will the heathen believe ?

The ambassadorial files contain many records of miracles performed and, for the heartening of younger members of the Service, the files are kept in order and up to date, for their perusal strengthens faith and revives hope.

Under the section " China " one may read of the proud, bigoted Confucian scholar, Hsi Sheng Mo, driven by poverty to the house of David Hill in the Chinese city of Ping Yang Fu, and there meeting with Christ's Envoy and instinctively recognising his nobility :

" One look, one word, was enough. As daylight banishes darkness, so did David Hill's presence dissipate all the idle rumours I had heard. All sense of fear was gone, my mind was at rest. I beheld his kindly eye, and remembered the words of Mencius : ' If a man's heart is not right, his eye will certainly bespeak it.' "

The signs following were such that Hsi himself became a faithful believer and an Ambassador of reconciliation. While he had breath, he preached the Gospel, healed the sick and cast out demons. He travelled many thousands of miles to declare the wonders of the new life and everywhere he won his fellow-countrymen to Christ.

The section " North Africa " supplies the following : " About one mile out of Casablanca (Morocco) is a colony known as Tin Town, where two thousand huts, knocked together from packing-cases and covered with old tin, sprawl across the sides of two low hills. Petrol tins, grease tins and all the tin refuse of a great commercial city has been patiently flattened into amazing tenements which now shelter ten thousand human beings.

" Traversed under a summer sun, when the flaming heat beats down on the littered refuse and human filthiness, among which bands of unkempt children romp and shout, the settlement nauseates by the forceful impact of its primitive animality.

" At nightfall, men, defaced in soul and body by sinful living, beaten in life's struggle, and crushed in the grip of hopeless poverty, slink into its dens to sleep.

" People die freely in Tin Town and a roomy cemetery lies quite close to it. Death in a rusty tin shack, set down in a pestilential lane in this settlement, in the horrid gloom of night, stirs the imagination. Native quacks and charm writers who deal in mummery and Koranic magic, do a thriving business of spoliation, but two missionary women carry on medical work there and are trusted by those who seek their help.

" In this place there is one Christian—a woman.

" Her strong, swarthy features, set off with coils of black hair, mark her south-land origin. In her tin tenement is a tiny garden, where sweet mint grows. Christ's miracle of grace has made a difference, a startling difference. Seated on the floor, amid a knot of her Moslem women neighbours, her gravity, reserve and Christian graciousness emphasise by contrast the surrounding sin and squalor."

Under " India " it is recorded how a proud boy from a noble home in the Punjab, entered a mission school, but flared into open rebellion on being compelled to read the Christian Scriptures. Rather than receive religious instruction under compulsion, he left the school and became ringleader of a hostile gang which threw mud and stones at the preachers. His final protest was publicly to burn copies of the Gospels. At that same hour the miracle began and questionings so disturbed his mind that a few days later he determined that unless he could find some answer to his problems, he would take his life.

That night he saw Christ, became His bond-servant and found in Him the answer to all his perplexities.

That youth became known to the world as the Christian Sadhu, Sundar Singh.

The file " Africa " tells of the missionary who, crossing tropical deserts, saw a negro, black in heart as in body, tilling a field baked as hard as a brick in the long drought. To his greeting and to his commiseration for the intractability of the land, came back a gruff blasphemy : " Yes ! A hard God has hardened the soil by denying rain."

Ten years later the same missionary greets the same man in the same field, now soaked soft by two days' rain. The blessing of refreshing showers has been bestowed, but also the miracle of new birth has been wrought and this time it is a Christian African who calls back : " Truly soft," says he, " is the soil, for the God Who softened my heart also softened the hard soil. He rained on my hard soul as well as on my parched field."

The folio " South India," sub-section " Children," holds the report of many signs that might be related for stimulating courage. Let one suffice, that of the child so gay in her dress that she seemed like a bird from the woods among the green shadows of the mango trees on the Christian compound.

Might she stay a while and learn a little ? No. Her Hindu father would have died rather than break his caste, so her pleading was in vain and into heathendom she was thrust, to live the shut-in life of her caste rule until, a seventeen-year-old bride, she left her parents' home for her husband's house.

Not one Scripture did she know, not one friend or

teacher was there to help her, she was illiterate and books were of no use to her. It might well be said that she knew nothing, but the spiritual conquered all in her and though she was walled in, she could never be roofed in.

The miracle-working God Himself taught her to trust, taught her to pray, taught her to take her daily bread from His hand, gave her life from the dead, sustained it in the face of every difficulty, and led her at last to the place where there were friends and fellowship and love and baptism.

Such instances could be quoted *ad infinitum*. The marvels have happened, are happening and will go on happening. What of personal responsibility ?

The things waiting to be done are so numerous, the claims so manifold, the demands so varied, that each man's contribution looks pitifully inadequate. Yet small as it is, each contribution is an essential part of the whole.

There is the record of Hsi Sheng Mo, but what of the scholars in China to-day ?

Men talk of Sundar Singh, but who is called to work among the schoolboys of India ?

We read of the negro in Africa ; whose personal responsibility is he ?

Where are the lovers of the Lord who should care for the children of the East ?

The state of the Christless world and the magnitude of the Church's task in relation to it, is overwhelming. To mention only a few of the facts :

There is the challenge of the Amazon Indians. " Spiritually they present a dark picture, living in perpetual fear of demons. A small beginning has been made to master their language, which promises to be difficult."

"Among the Berbers of the Middle Atlas, the soldiers of the State have already prepared the way. Shall the servants of the Lord be wanting there with the message of Light?"

"From among the hill folk of North-East Siam comes the urgent call 'the King's business requireth haste.'"

A Central Asian pioneer sat with a prisoner in his cage that he might learn from him the Kalmuk dialect, and prepare books for that people. Now he has died. Who is ready to carry on that work?

Who has considered the needs of the Nomad Yezidis of Northern Iraq, who are spoken of as the "Chosen People of the Fallen Angel" and whose women are deprived of all human rights?

An appeal has come for the Mozabites of the Sahara, among whose villages the visitor walks through silent roads, and between windowless houses. "Behind those closed doors the girls are growing up literally locked away."

The League of Nations Report on "Traffic in Women and Children in the Far East," states that the number of Russian refugees leading dissolute lives under stress of destitution in North China and Manchuria, has become a notorious scandal.

No single Christian in this land is free of responsibility concerning the Christless world at our doors, the slum areas of England, the destitute children of our cities, the cynical prostitutes, the heathen of the docks and all the scum of the seething cauldron of our modern social system.

Who is ready for an appointment to rescue the perishing of this country ? Who will go to the Black Zone of Paris ? To Tin Town in Morocco ? To a Leper Settlement ? To the Untouchables of India ? To the segregated women of the harem ? To the Geisha girls of Japan ?

Who is willing for life in Eastern inns where dirt and vermin are accepted as normal conditions; in nomad tents where the food is sun-dried yak flesh, sour milk and rancid butter which must be accepted with a grace equal to that of the man who offers it; in towns which have no sanitation, where water is scarce and where flies settle like a black veil on the sticky table and on the food, rising with a sickening buzz when disturbed.

All this and much more awaits the recruit, yet he will find it literally true that the pinpricks of this present are not worthy to be compared with the over-weight of joy that is his in Christ's ambassadorial service.

Can the gigantic task ever be accomplished ? Yes, it can, but only if every man be at his appointed post.

Some excuse themselves, saying : " I have no call," when what they really mean is that they never heard the call, probably because they never expected to receive one. When a man is expecting to receive his designation he must be tuned in to the Divine otherwise he may never even hear God speak, and in the din of the world's jazz may miss his commission altogether.

" Therefore take heed how ye hear ! "

" It was well that it was in Thine Heart "

"WE have carefully considered your case and have very regretfully reached the conclusion that we cannot accept you for foreign service."

The Secretary of the Missionary Society was exceedingly kind and tried to say helpful things, but it was a heavy blow and it shattered a whole edifice of hopes. For the second time this recruit had been rejected by a Mission Board.

He had felt so sure that he was right in offering himself, and every circumstance had seemed to justify him in going forward. He knew himself medically fit and felt confident that his references had been satisfactory. In fact no definite objection had been raised and when he applied he was accepted for training and had spent one year in the Society's Training College.

During that period he had done his best to measure up, but the whole time he was uncomfortably conscious that the atmosphere was not wholly congenial to him and that he was not fitting in happily with the other students. Nothing serious, but he realised quite well that, temperamentally, he was not an easy man to get on with.

He always envied others their capacity for facile intercourse, but all his life he had been shy, self-conscious and awkward—" dour," his Scotch associates called him. He had never made a friend, but in the office, though he was not popular and though he went his own way leaving others to go theirs, no friction ever occurred.

In Church life he was valued and gave many hours each week to assist the minister with accounts and with the business side of the work. He never undertook to give help in special evangelistic efforts, for his gifts did not lie that way.

When the Missionary Society in which he was interested and to which he subscribed, issued an urgent appeal for volunteers, he took it very seriously and this offer of service had been his response. It was not an easy step to take, but he braced himself to it. He never could take things lightly, and if the need were as great as they said, he must volunteer whatever it meant, and it meant a great deal.

The Board of the first Society to which he applied, told him that they did not happen to require a man with business training just then, and that he had not the necessary qualifications for other posts. So that was that.

Having gone so far he could not drop the matter, because it was not in his nature to start on a venture and fail to carry it through. Therefore three months later he made another application, this time to a Society of a different order. He realised this when he saw the papers, for the leading questions were all drafted in view of drawing out information regarding the candidate's spiritual history.

He knew that his answers sounded a little dry, but he had no thrilling experiences to tell and nothing would induce him to colour them up for the sake of gaining approbation. As for leading men to Christ, well, he had his own way of doing this and it did not look impressive, when he put it down in black and white.

This time he was accepted on probation. For a whole year he had done his best to fit in, though he always felt like a square peg in a round hole. Now he must take the refusal as final and go back to office work, and to his old duties at the Church. He knew he was a lucky man to have a job waiting for him and it was a great consolation, at this painful hour, to realise that the man who knew him best wanted him back.

He was ever a thinker and a ponderer of problems. During the months that followed he could never rid his mind of the question : " Was I really called by God, or did I follow a will o' the wisp, sent out to lead me astray?" He could not see his way through it; all he knew was that he had made the only move possible to an honourable Christian man who hears of a great need which it is perhaps in his power to meet. The whole experience left him neither bitter nor resentful, but profoundly puzzled.

He meditated : " If I were dealing with anyone who had good intentions and only desired to do the right thing, I should see to it that he knew what the right thing was, and what I wanted him to do. I would not let him flounder, nor would I let him make a mistake. If it were at the office, my orders to him would be quite clear and definite. Have we not the right to expect Divine guidance to be equally straightforward ? "

He continued for a long time in this puzzled mood but in the end illumination came, and this is the way in which it came.

There was a change of *personnel* at the office and it
brought promotion for him. His new position made
a quite different demand on his powers. So far his
had been routine work but now he was admitted to
the council where plans, projects and ventures were
discussed. He saw how he had hitherto worked in
a small, water-tight compartment where he had been
little more than an efficient machine. The action and
reaction of that department was fixed and there was
no room for uncertainty or for venture.

Now all was different and every day surprising
things happened; allowance had always to be made
for the unexpected. The new life was one of endeavour, speculation and adventure. He was suddenly transferred from the position of a man in a
restricted sphere, who works for the thing visible
and tangible, to another plane altogether. Any
instructions which now reached him came in quite
different terms. It used to be, " Do this," and he
did it; but now he was entrusted with the knowledge
of aims, purposes and objectives, but was not always
told in detail how to attain them.

One day while pondering his old problem of
guidance, something clicked in his mind, and in a
flash he saw that it was not incompatible with the
final purpose of his life that he should have been led
to offer for foreign service and have been rejected.
Indeed it might well be a mere incident relative to
far wider issues.

Here in this business house, the inexperienced
clerk was occupied with the detail of the immediate
and was not concerned with broader purposes. As
promotion came, however, his horizons were widened

and he instinctively looked to the end on which all
the detail work was focussed.

With this in mind he read with new illumination of
Abraham, obeying God to the point of binding his
son on the altar, and then being stopped by the Voice ;
of Moses, brought within sight of the Promised Land
and then refused admittance ; of Job, exalted to an
eminence, then cast down to a dung-hill ; of David,
commended for wishing to build a house for God
and encouraged by the prophet to do so, then stopped
in his purpose.   Perhaps this word which God spoke
to David was the key to the perplexing problem :
" It was well that it was in thine heart."

He saw it now.   Men who were to handle things of
spiritual import, who were to reckon with the unseen,
had lessons to learn in a school where every detail was
not immediately made plain.   It was for them to be so
confident of the Guide and so certain of His leading
that there could be no clamouring for explanations.

In view of the special service to which he was later
called, he recognised, in the incident of his two
offers to the Missionary Societies, and their refusal
of his help, a sure and certain sign to himself and to
others that everything had been laid upon the altar.
By doing so he had gained freedom, for his obedience
was established both to himself and to his friends.
He had withheld nothing that was asked of him.

He now knew that the service required of him was
to be Christ's witness in one of England's great
industrial centres.   A glorious calling !   He sometimes wondered if any man on the foreign mission
field had such scope as he, and he rejoiced increasingly
in the commission entrusted to him.

He recalled the effect of the appeal issued by the Missionary Society and so forcibly emphasised by the deputation. It made a volunteer of him. The claims of his own country were no less insistent. How was it that no voice of equal authority presented them? What of the Christian man's commission to be a voice for God in Parliament, to raise His standard in the Law Courts, to magnify Him in a scholastic career, to stand for rectitude in business and for purity in journalism. What of the need to occupy every available post in prisons, reformatories and hospitals and fill them with men and women whose first business was witness and who had no reservations in the wholeheartedness of their service?

He had attended so many missionary meetings and heard so many appeals but they were always for the foreign field, and he observed that directly a young man showed special keenness in things spiritual it was assumed that he must become a foreign missionary. He could not remember hearing one definite appeal from the pulpit urging the young to prepare themselves to capture pivotal posts in their own land with the definite view of holding them for Christ.

What was the matter? Did the Church not covet these strategic appointments sufficiently to make an effort to secure them? If the children of light were so apathetic, the children of darkness were not.

The field was the world, and he held his business appointment in it under as direct a commission from the Lord of the harvest as any missionary pioneer of distant lands.

The Ambassador on Leave

THERE was an unusual stir in Venice one Sunday
afternoon and crowds made their way to the
beautiful Church which stood out so picturesquely
against the deep blue sky. The men and women
seemed unconscious of the beauty around them, of
the canals, the gondolas, the musicians and the holiday
makers, for they were pressing to a missionary meeting
where they were to see again one of their own people
who, years ago, had gone to China. Some had
known him as a child, and to all he was in the saintly
succession of those who might yet win the martyr's
crown.

By the time the great bell had ceased to toll the
Church was packed with standing people. Vespers
were ornate that day for the officiating prelate had
come direct from Rome, bearing the Pontifical blessing
to five young Franciscans who were shortly to leave
for the East.

When the preacher came forward the crowd fell
back to make way for him to reach the pulpit. His
was a striking figure for he wore Chinese dress and
a round Chinese cap on his head and by every movement and gesture was Chinese. So perfectly had he

adjusted his ways to the land of his adoption that he seemed the replica of a figure on a Chinese vase, but when he opened his mouth he was an Italian, and as he spoke of the joys and sorrows of a missionary's life, the flowing speech of his exuberant race poured forth to describe his experiences. He spoke first of the Boxer riots and of the massacre of his beloved friend, companion and fellow-priest. Tears poured down his cheeks and a sob caught his voice which was echoed by the emotional crowd. Then he told of the nostalgia and the longing for home, for vineyards, olive groves and Tuscan villages, which tugs at the exile's heart. As he closed there was a murmur of sympathy from the congregation, which was stilled as the five young monks came forward and knelt at the altar, afterwards to be embraced by the prelate and to have the Pope's scapula hung round their necks.

Then each young Franciscan took an offertory plate and walked out into the crowd to receive the gifts of the people. As they moved about, the congregation pressed upon them and flung money into the large platters, fearful lest they lose the chance of giving and miss their share in the offering.

As the romantic-looking youths walked past, a storm of emotion burst forth in the audience. Already dedicated to a life of loneliness and hardship they were now to sail for a foreign land from which they would almost certainly never return. The pathos of this thought stirred the congregation to a high pitch of religious fervour. Sobs and cries broke out and blessings were invoked on their

young and holy heads. *Dio mio ! Santa Maria !
Poverini !*

In a few days they would leave Italy and the glorious
setting of Venice, the cathedral of San Marco, the
blue Adriatic, the green vineyards, the fruits and
flowers of their beloved land would be left behind
for ever, for in the book of instructions issued to its
missionaries the Roman Catholic Church quite clearly
states that the missionary must die in the land to
which he is sent. " It is hard, but it is his duty," and
it was the unusual sight of a missionary back for a
period in his own land that was stirring Venice.

The pains of nostalgia are very real to the missionary,
and there is a subconscious longing for the old scenes,
for the accustomed life, for friends and for the simple
pleasures of home, but these are transient griefs and
the old warrior seldom gives them place. The real
sorrows are of quite another order. They are not in
the realm of the emotions but on the spiritual plane,
and from the hour when he sails the missionary
becomes in a very real sense a pilgrim who has no
fixed abode and no certain dwelling-place, nor will
he ever find one until he enters the city which has
foundations, whose Builder and Maker is God.

The Catholic missionary has a deeper cut but a
cleaner scar, for the wound is not periodically re-
opened as is that of the Protestant, whose wound
bleeds afresh every time he tears himself away from
one side or the other.

The Protestant Church views the question of furlough from quite a different angle to the Catholic.
It desires that its missionaries should be as little
removed from the normal as possible and to this end

wishes to bring them periodically into touch with home conditions. In this way links of friendship, of interest, and of sympathy with the home Church are never wholly severed and the home constituency has an opportunity of gaining first-hand information about all parts of the foreign field. Moreover, the health of the missionary is benefited and those who have had a more specialised training are afforded the opportunity of post-graduate courses.

Furlough is a psychological crisis. An individual has become absorbed into a life on which demands are made by a dependent people which keep it pouring out ceaselessly through every channel of communication. When the word reaches him : " Your furlough is due. Your passage is taken to leave in two months' time," every root has to be torn up, and the Easterners' tender dependence makes this period of uprooting as painful as possible.

However, it is done, and the missionary, once set going, moves from scene to scene until he has crossed the world and realises that within twenty-four hours he will be among his own people again.

What that last day and night mean to him, is known only to those who have gone through it. The anticipation, the apprehension, the hope, the dread, the joy, the terror, the confidence of welcome and the nervousness of reunion. Sometimes parents whose children have passed from childhood to adolescence since they last met, have to brace themselves to the meeting and they do so with mingled joy and pain. Contemporaries who should normally have grown older together suffer from the jar of attempting to meet on the old footing after a separation of years.

Losses and changes which have occurred have not been met one by one, but are to be encountered all at once and must come with overwhelming force. Sometimes a young man brings home a wife and children who are strangers to the home circle, and he asks himself what impression will be made and whether they will fit in happily.

The boat draws slowly to the wharf. The gangway is lowered and a moment later his own people and old friends surround him and carry him off. The plunge is taken and he emerges to find that things are much easier than he anticipated.

The next few weeks are usually very happy and are spent in renewing old ties and seeing familiar places. Then comes the period when the first flutter of excitement is over and the missionary has to decide how the year of leave is to be spent.

The society to which he belongs will require of him a quota of his time for what it calls " deputation work," which is the job of visiting Churches and centres for the purpose of reporting on his work and so informing the constituency and rousing their interest, that support will be forthcoming.

If he be a wise man he will see to it that his report is so given that the minds of his hearers will not be narrowed down to interest in his personal work, *his* school, *his* station, *his* hospital, but that their outlook will be enlarged to perceive wider horizons so that, looking on the field, they will grasp the importance of the general situation and rouse themselves to take their part in the purpose of God for the world.

He will find that they are most easily moved by the recital of intimate detail and incidents in the lives of the natives and will be most willing to contribute money for the support of a child or evangelist whose photograph can be supplied to them and whom they come to regard to some extent as their personal property. Such interest is local, temporary and of little value, and his part is to teach them to lift up their eyes and look on the field and hold themselves ready both by prayer and gifts to make a contribution when and how it may be needed.

The missionary may not be a very effective speaker and the work in which he has been engaged may not be of a very striking character, but that is immaterial. He must have general knowledge of missions on a much wider basis than his own personal work, and he must be competent to answer the questions which are asked by intelligent people. If he be going to impart a broad outlook he must have a broad outlook himself. He must take time and trouble over every address he gives. Laziness accounts for most of the dry missionary speeches, for the recital of the contacts of Christ with the human soul, and the progress or conflict at the front is a stream of interest that never fails.

Let him study the writings of a certain Doctor called Luke and see how local colour can be so adroitly applied that the incident is impressed by the detail of its setting and points its own moral.

It is not, however, in meetings that his most important work will be done. Kind, generous people will open their houses to him and he should by this time have learnt the gentle art of being a guest. He may be the foreign missionary and for the time being a centre of interest, but the affairs of his host and hostess are just as important as his own. He is there to help people enlarge their vision; let them help him to enlarge his. He must take time for contacts and be courteous, accessible, discreet and tactful.

The native Church and its problems loom large in his mind and when strangers ask a question as to what his work has been, he is apt to pour forth a wealth of information, for which he soon finds that neither clergy nor laity have any thirst, and though they will all give him a sympathetic hearing at whatever meeting they have arranged for him to take, even his best friends are not concerned with the missionary problems which fill his own thoughts.

Away in the jungle he has largely become a man of one idea, and his friends' indifference to that idea makes him conscious of a great loneliness which is only dispelled by seizing every occasion of meeting with others of his own calling. With them he talks of little else but missionary news and native Church difficulties. Even association with men who have been in other countries does not give the same pleasure as meeting with those from his own part of the field. In the gatherings at his own Mission headquarters he always finds, besides men on furlough like himself, seniors now holding posts at home and veterans retired from active service. They gather from suburbs and country towns for the sake of talking Africa, India, or China, together, and he sees in them the same craving to ventilate missionary topics as he finds in himself.

So the year passes and not without relief does he see the season come round which is the signal to return to that distant land. The last few months have brought him one very difficult experience and he has even come to dread the sight of the overseas mail, for it brings letters from the man who holds his post during this furlough. At first all went well and there was appreciative reference to " the warm reception given us by the dear Christians of Yakada." A little later the same man was " sorry to report that money which the Christians had undertaken to raise locally toward the expenses of the mission school has not been forthcoming. This was a surprise to us after all we had heard of the fine, independent work and spirit of self-support among your people."

Immediately following on this were other complaints involving individual converts and centring on one man who was suspected of causing much of the trouble. " I know how highly you thought of Philip, but I am sorry to tell you that we have come to the conclusion that he is not as reliable in money matters as you believed him to be. I brought my evangelist here with me and he has found out that Philip used a substantial sum of mission money for himself. For the sake of the native Church I have decided to exclude him from taking part in any Church services."

The man on furlough found this letter lying on his breakfast table—he seized and read it, then turned from his untouched food and went back to his room, where he prayed in agony of soul for this convert whose weaknesses he knew full well but whom he loved as a parent loves a child. The winning of that soul had cost him much and he felt that the hour when the man most needed him he could give him no help. Meanwhile this *locum* and his pet evangelist might easily succeed in antagonising him so that he would finally be alienated from Christianity.

This was bad enough, but a fortnight later he suffered such pain that the remainder of his leave was spoilt by it. At a missionary meeting in a country town he had, as usual, spoken of his work and of the local church which, as a result, had come into being. At the close of the meeting a lady came to him and said :

" I am so much interested to meet you, for the man who is taking your place has married my daughter. They have had a very difficult time and have been badly let down over Philip. It must be a blow to you to find how untrustworthy he is. My daughter also tells me that the women of the Church are cold and rather unsatisfactory."

He restrained himself with difficulty from telling the woman what he thought of her, her daughter, her son-in-law and his mischief-making evangelist.

" Cold, indeed ! " he said to himself; " put them in an icehouse and then blame them for being chilled."

He controlled himself but went away sore and feeling that for once he did well to be angry. He was indignant with the missionary who could so far forget himself as to break every rule of loyalty and discretion in Christ's ambassadorial service. Here was a convert whom he loved and over whom he had prayed and wrestled, a man whose background of sorrow and tragedy he alone knew and his reported sin was now spoken of as lightly as though that immortal soul were merely the number on a pigeon hole. It was quite possible that the whole accusation was a lie, concocted by some enemy, but already it had become the talk of British provincial tea-parties.

As far as rest of spirit was concerned that day ended furlough for him, and when, three months later, he went back and took over the tragic muddle of a mishandled situation, he thought : " One of the greatest values of furlough might be that it should be made the occasion to leave to the native Church, all matters of administration and responsibility. Mistakes of inexperience could probably be easily rectified, and in some cases the experiment might work so well that the missionary himself need never again take over those particular duties, and would thus find himself released for his more legitimate work of evangelism."

Physically he was well and passed the doctor with flying colours after a most careful medical examination. During his last interview with the Board, though much was said about the recuperation of his physical being, there was no mention of the recreation of his mind and no enquiry as to his spiritual fitness.

Mentally and spiritually, furlough had not been the benefit to him that it should have been. He had forgotten something that was said to him in the Training College : " Beware of ruts ; they are really shallow graves. You will never wholly escape them on the field, but use your furlough to dig yourself out. Get back to the normal by seizing all the mental recreation which has been denied you for years. Mix with ordinary men and talk with them on general subjects. Take a change—learn, don't teach—get back into touch with contemporary life. Look at beautiful works of art. Hear good music, exercise your intelligence at good lectures, and when you go back to your station and your missionary circle, take with you a better-equipped mind than [you brought home.

" As to the spiritual, seeing that the main business of your life is to impart spiritual things, let it be the main business of your furlough to be refreshed in the realm of the spirit. If you have grown, as you should have grown, you need something very different from that which you enjoyed ten years earlier."

It is stimulating to worship with large congregations and helpful to store the mind with memories of song and prayer, but Bible Study is the strong food which the missionary requires. His danger is lest he merely gather with the crowd to enjoy a helpful discourse, while what he needs, is suggestive teaching of so deep a nature that it costs him hours of solid thought to explore the new avenues open to him.

No missionary on leave is without shame that he so poorly represents his Lord, and without humiliation at the poverty of his spiritual equipment. Remembering it, he asks himself how he dare hold a place in so sacred a service and many a time, when the crowd is shut out, he meditates on the love and forbearance of the Saviour Who condescends to send him out once more.

He dare not return unless re-commissioned. The glamour helped him on his first going forth, but this time the naked difficulty of his task faces him in utter realism. He now knows the loneliness, the weariness, the hardness of the heathen, the possible instability of converts, the ingratitude of those he would help, and the lack of understanding in the very people who need him most. Yet with the re-commission comes the confidence that all the resources of God are at his disposal and, in hope born of experience, he takes up his work again.

Looking back, he sees himself starting out for the first time, taking obstacles with the energy of youth and making as little of them as does the babbling brook of the pebbles that would impede its course. This time there is less noise, but he is conscious of a tremendous power which carries him forward and which he can only compare with the force of a boundless ocean. That force is the will of God which has become the sole purpose of his undivided heart.

Finally the re-commissioning, as the first appointment, demands quiet and silence, when other voices are shut out while the Ambassador takes his new instructions.

The Splendour of the Ambassy

THE word " splendour " immediately calls up the picture of the sun in all its glory, an orb the rays of which disseminate light, warmth and vitalising force through space.

Splendour of the Missionary Calling? What connection has this word with the laborious, arduous, patient toil of a missionary life?

The reader has seen that the missionary, must above all, be single-eyed, disciplined, determined, purposeful, self-forgetful, persevering and obedient. He must serve without reservation, and may make no terms regarding his pay, his designation, his promotion or his rewards. In fact the terms of his service militate against prestige or material splendour.

The universe being God's handiwork its solar systems are perfect illustrations of the relationship between Christ and His disciples which He expressed as " I am the Light—Ye are the Light." He is the whole light, but as the rays convey and exhibit the light of the sun, so His disciples exhibit His light and glory to the world.

As the sole honour of Christ's Ambassador lies in the fact that he directly represents his King, so also his only splendour consists in being the visible expression of his Sovereign's majesty.

The Splendour of the Ambassy

His abode, be it a grass-roofed hut in tropical Africa, a shack in China, a snow-house in the Arctic or a tent in the burning desert, is The Residency over which waves the banner of his King and round which an angel guard keeps watch.

This must ever be holy ground, even though all around be evil, for the Embassy is privileged land and here the Ambassador enjoys extra-territorial rights. No one may interfere in the correspondence and intercourse between him and his King. He is supplied with wireless communication which can never be tampered with by the enemy nor ever confiscated, whatever the condition of the country.

His intercourse with his sovereign is so safeguarded that no spy can overhear his reports or intercept his dispatches. At any moment of the day or night he may have audience with his King, secure His counsel, receive His instructions and can never fail of His understanding sympathy. He may report freely concerning all things at any time and never suffer a moment's delay to his audience. "His ear is ever open unto their cry."

His court dress needs no human tailoring to keep it in repair. It is of fine linen which must be kept white and clean so that in the execution of his daily business his spotless raiment will be a cause of wonder to men whose garments are always defiled by the mire of the streets. To this end he has hourly access to the fountain which is open for sin and for uncleanness and has no excuse for trailing soiled apparel. He can never be starved out for he is supplied with the bread of life, and there is a well of living water from which he may drink at all times.

In fact he enjoys all the privileges which belong to those who represent the Court of Heaven on earth and these privileges can be compared with nothing in this world.

He carries everywhere a personal letter from his King which is full of encouragement and cheer and it bears a seal on which are stamped the words: " Remember I am with you always, day by day."

Sometimes the splendour of his commission will flood the Ambassador with glory but not always, and his chief vigilance is directed on how to detect the insidious infiltration of the commonplace into his life. Once there it intensifies the material at the expense of the unseen, and gradually robs his calling of all its glory.

" The Residency ? " What, this dingy house always filled with a sick, ragged and exacting crowd ?

" An angel guard ? " Why, some have been killed !

" Direct audience ? " When prayer brings no response ?

How to live in, yet be not of, this sordid, impure and falsely-valued world which he must use but not be used by, live in but only as a wayfarer, look on but as one wholly undeceived by its lies, is his chief care.

Were he left alone the world would be too much for him but he has a Friend, a Comforter, a Remembrancer, a Strengthener, an Adviser, Who abides with him in closest intimacy and this Friend is the Lord of Glory. When He illumines the everyday things of life, and they are touched again with His golden ray the Ambassador's service is caught once more within a noose of light.

The Ambassador receives his Passport

On the outskirts of the Forum Romanum is a building among the foundations of which lies a dungeon where, in dense darkness, the condemned prisoners of the Cæsars spent the last hours before they were led out to execution. There now remains in it only one erect iron post and a fragment of the chain to which the last prisoner was bound.

Every kind of criminal found his way to that cell, but once a condemned man went there because he was a servant of the Most High God and an Ambassador for Christ. This man was used to prisons and had seen such miracles occur as that an earthquake once shook the building and set him free. But this time nothing of that kind happened.

On the morning of the day of execution day broke, but no ray of the rising sun could pierce the gloom of the condemned cell. This was the last day on earth for Paul the aged. In a few hours he was to take his last walk outside the city gate of Rome. He would go out but not come back, because at a certain point his spirit would be liberated from the body, and the enemy who had for so long vent his fury on him, would give one final thrust and then have no more that he could do.

For on the day when the body dies, the rebel king must needs stand aside to give him free exit from the sphere of his appointment to the Courts of his Fatherland. This veteran Envoy had finished his course, he had kept the faith and now was recalled to receive his reward and perhaps a new position where he would exercise wider powers than he had yet dreamt of.

He had so tirelessly besought men to be reconciled to God, so skilfully pleaded the claims of his King, so insistently witnessed to the liberating power of the all-conquering Christ, so fearlessly exposed the strategies of the powers of darkness, that the legions of hell had gnashed upon him in fury and sought by every subterfuge, to silence his witness.

Just where Paul's blood was spilled they built a church to mark the spot and in it they wrote the words :

" To me to live is Christ—To die is gain,"

but the cold, rigid, marble building only marks the spot where the body fell, while the real edifice which commemorates St. Paul, is that company of men and women who, in true apostolic succession, have ever since been Ambassadors of the Court of Heaven.

As each envoy's service comes to a close he receives a summons. The hour when it comes may find him in a dungeon, but more likely in some Indian or Chinese city, in a tropical jungle, among Communist brigands, on an ice-bound Himalayan Pass or in an Asian Desert. Perhaps even in his own land surrounded by loved ones.

In the final issue the where is of no moment. The

command has come and must be obeyed. He is called home and the antagonist who has flouted, mocked, tormented and persecuted him has done his worst. The Ambassador now crosses the frontier to his own *patria* where he is welcomed and where joys and honour await him.

As he sets his foot in that other country he is transfigured and has raiment put on him that glistens white as snow.

All the bells in the city ring out for joy and it is said to him : " Well done, good and faithful servant, enter thou into the joy of thy Lord ! "

So he goes in and sees his King.

Epilogue

" ALL authority in heaven and on earth has been
given to Me. Go therefore and make disciples of
all the nations; baptise them into the name of the
Father, and of the Son and of the Holy Spirit; and
teach them to observe every commandment which I
have given you. And remember, I am with you
always, day by day, until the Close of the Age."

" Whom shall I send and who will go for Us ? "
" Here am I; send me."

" Can you drink out of the cup from which I am
about to drink ? " said Jesus.
" We can," they replied.
" You shall drink out of My cup," He said.

" And they went out and preached everywhere,
the Lord working with them and confirming their
message by the signs which accompanied it."

" They were stoned, they were sawn asunder,
they were tried by temptation, they were killed with
the sword. They went from place to place in sheep-
skins or goatskins, enduring want, oppression, and

cruelty . . . they wandered across deserts and mountains, or hid themselves in caves and in holes in the ground."

" Who shall separate us from Christ's love? Shall affliction or distress, persecution or hunger, nakedness or danger or the sword? . . . For I am convinced that neither death nor life, nor angels nor sovereignties, nor things present nor things future, nor powers nor height nor depth, nor any other created thing shall be able to separate us from the love of God which is in Christ Jesus our Lord."

" After this I beheld and lo a great multitude which no man could number, of all nations, and kindreds, and people, and tongues, stood before the throne, and before the Lamb, clothed with white robes, and palms in their hands ; and cried with a loud voice, saying, Salvation to our God which sitteth upon the throne and unto the Lamb."

" And there shall be no more curse but the throne of God and of the Lamb shall be in it ; and His servants shall serve Him; and they shall see His face; and His name shall be in their foreheads . . . and they shall reign for ever and ever."

THE END

11449

THIS BOOK MAY B

14 Days

and may be renewed if not called
someone else.
A fine of per day is charged if the book
is kept after the last date stamped below.

DUE	DUE	DUE

OCT 25 200

FEB 16

SEP 30 '66

'69